THE SCIENCE
of SUCCESS

THE SCIENCE
of SUCCESS

―――――

NAPOLEON HILL

Foreword and Compilation by Judith Williamson

AN OFFICIAL PUBLICATION OF THE
NAPOLEON HILL FOUNDATION

JEREMY P. TARCHER/PENGUIN
a member of Penguin Group (USA)
New York

JEREMY P. TARCHER/PENGUIN
Published by the Penguin Group
Penguin Group (USA) LLC
375 Hudson Street
New York, New York 10014

USA • Canada • UK • Ireland • Australia
New Zealand • India • South Africa • China

penguin.com
A Penguin Random House Company

Most Tarcher/Penguin books are available at special quantity discounts for bulk purchase for sales promotions, premiums, fund-raising, and educational needs. Special books or book excerpts also can be created to fit specific needs. For details, write: Special.Markets@us.penguingroup.com.

Library of Congress Cataloging-in-Publication Data

Hill, Napoleon, 1883–1970.
[Essays. Selections]
The science of success: Napoleon Hill's proven program for prosperity and happiness / Napoleon Hill.
p.   cm.—(Tarcher success classics)
ISBN 978-0-399-17095-9
1. Success.   2. Success in business.   I. Title.
HF5386.H5634   2014   2014015577
650.1—dc23

Printed in the United States of America
1   3   5   7   9   10   8   6   4   2

CONTENTS

Part Three: Additional
Science of Success Series Lessons

NAPOLEON HILL

THE MAN AND HIS MESSAGE

From the Editors of
SUCCESS MAGAZINE

FOREWORD

The *Science of Success* is a publication of previously uncollected works that appeared throughout Dr. Hill's lifetime in newspapers and special edition magazines.

These articles by reporters and Dr. Hill offer added insight into the author's popularity and engaging style as both a motivational speaker and a writer.

I find that the real treasure trove exists in the Science of Success series that includes the 35 *Miami Herald* articles and the additional 18 in-depth essays detailing the success principles, one concept at a time.

As a student, practitioner, instructor, and educational director of the Napoleon Hill World Learning Center for Dr. Hill's Success Philosophy, I always look forward to finding additional writings that he himself penned. In these newspaper columns, Dr. Hill uses many of the same concepts that appeared in his other writings but with different illustrations to drive home his points and make them understandable by anyone.

For everyone who has enjoyed Dr. Hill's books, these new and uncollected articles demonstrate the proliferation of his influence worldwide, across cultures, and in varying secular and religious denominations. He truly cuts across many boundaries to get the word out on how to achieve personal success.

Begin by reading these offerings as an introduction to Dr. Hill's lifetime works. Next, consider going a little deeper by reading one or more of his classic works, such as *Think and Grow Rich*, *Law of Success*, or *How to Sell Your Way Through Life*. Simultaneously, begin putting into action what Dr. Hill discusses in each article.

The purpose here is not to "conform" to what Dr. Hill writes about, but to "perform" his script in your own life for your ultimate success.

At the onset, consider working with one or two of the ideas that appeal to you, and then when you see concrete results of so doing, add another of Dr. Hill's teachings and begin to build a formidable foundation for success in your own life. As you witness what happens, I predict that you will eagerly let your old self stand aside and introduce your new and improved "higher self" to the world.

As either an introduction or as a refresher course in Dr. Hill's philosophy, this book will serve you equally well.

The short essays are engaging, easy to read aloud for emphasis, and contain noteworthy sayings that can serve as affirmations, thought starters, or calls to action.

I surely enjoyed collecting the materials and compiling the book because it underscored for me the relevancy and practicality of Dr. Hill's ageless works. Dr. Hill recognized the timeless nature of his works when he spoke of their benefit "for future generations yet unborn."

I wholeheartedly recommend this book as required reading if you are a serious student and practitioner of Dr. Hill's Success Philosophy.

Be Your Very Best Always,
Judith Williamson

Part One

UNCOLLECTED WORKS

"The formula appears to be simple . . . it appears to be basic. Yet it represents the distilled effort of a lifetime."

THE MAN WHO TAUGHT
MILLIONS HOW TO SUCCEED

by John Johnson

There's hardly a person alive today who doesn't know of Napoleon Hill and his law of success. Millions of readers throughout the world have read and benefited from his teachings. Few, however, may be aware of the tremendous personal success of their author . . . a man who used his philosophy to rise from small town oblivion to international prominence. In this issue, "The Man Who Taught Millions How to Succeed" tells the fabulous story of his life and reveals how the formula he originated can bring success to you!

All Americans were inspired and stirred when they heard, in 1933, the resonant voice of Franklin Delano Roosevelt proclaim, "We have nothing to fear but fear itself." Men everywhere were electrified by this statement which brought a halt to the panic that had shattered our economy and had shaken the foundations of our government.

While the President spoke these words another man listened with quiet satisfaction. This man was accustomed to supplying words and ideas for others in every walk of life. Doing so was his life's work. The fact that the President of the United States saw fit to use the idea he, in his capacity as confidential advisor, had expressed was another milestone in a long and fruitful career dedicated to giving the world a philosophy that men could use to better themselves.

This man who remained anonymously in the shadows was Napoleon Hill. As the author of *Think and Grow Rich*, *How to Raise Your Own Salary*, and other best sellers, he might be considered a successful writer. But those who really understand the message he tries to convey recognize him as much more than just an author. Writing is only one of the instruments he has used to tell millions the truth about themselves and the powers they seldom realize that they possess.

What are these powers? Succinctly stated, they include vast and untapped reservoirs of human intelligence and ability. Hill has the distinction of having devoted his life to the creation of a formula which unleashes these powers with maximum force . . . and of teaching people how to apply his findings in their daily lives.

The voice of 65-year-old Napoleon Hill has been heard in every corner of the world . . . and its effects have been potent. Millions of readers in 20 foreign nations have read his books. Even far-off India has been stirred by his work. Through the influence of Mahatma Gandhi, a publisher in Bombay, India, publishes and distributes all of the Hill success books. In Brazil his books have been translated and published in the Portuguese language. And a special edition of his most popular book, *Think and Grow Rich*, was published in Sydney, Australia, and distributed throughout the British Empire. Although this book was first published in the United States in 1937, it is still a "best seller" throughout the nation, and huge numbers of copies of it have been purchased by employers as gifts for their employees.

Napoleon Hill started his quest for the formula of success early in life. When he found it, he shared his knowledge with waiting millions who otherwise might have remained shrouded in the obscurity from which they came.

His motivation for doing so can be found in the almost unbelievable story of his life. The son of an impoverished Virginia mountaineer, he seemed fated to spend his life wallowing in unrelieved ignorance. "Moonshiners, mountain stills, illiteracy, and deadly family feuds were the principal industries of our community," he says with a smile, "and the usual home was a crumbling clapboard shack or a dirt-floored cabin."

The Hills lived in a house of the latter description. When his mother died, young Napoleon, a name bestowed in honor of a rich paternal great uncle, was still a child. The blow left its mark. Probably to hide the scar, he achieved the distinction of being the toughest boy in Wise County. He wore it like a badge of honor—until his father presented the nine-year-old boy with a stepmother.

The new Mrs. Hill brought a fresh outlook into the

household. Not a mountaineer herself, she was appalled by what she found . . . and she was determined to change it. Napoleon, who could have been her biggest problem, turned into her greatest victory.

"I was introduced to her as the 'meanest' boy in town," the famed success-scientist recalls. "But my stepmother took one look at me and said, 'He's not the meanest boy. He's only a boy who hasn't learned how to direct his smartness to constructive ends.'" In a sense, these words were to become the cornerstone of the philosophy he was destined to develop in the decades that followed. Mrs. Hill became a guiding light. Using her dowry, she sent her husband to school and didn't rest until he was a successful dentist. Napoleon and his younger brother were rescued by her determination to give them a chance. At 12 the future inspirer of millions completed grade school; at 14 he was a part-time reporter for 15 newspapers, and at 15, after completing high school, he entered a business college at Tazewell, Virginia. As his horizons expanded, his abhorrence of ignorance grew and his determination to advance increased.

When he finished business college, he got a job with a leading attorney. How the callow 16-year-old managed to make the connection is a saga of audacity . . . and foresight. He reasoned that his first job should be a stepping-stone. A good start was essential and money, at this point, was almost unimportant.

Accordingly, he wrote a letter to Rufus A. Ayres, a former attorney general of Virginia and one of the state's most famous lawyers. The letter, in substance, said as follows:

I have just completed a business college course and am well-qualified to serve as your secretary, a position I am very anxious to have. Since I have no previous experience, I know that at the beginning of working for you will be of more value to me than it will be to you. Because of this, I am willing to pay for the privilege of working with you. You may charge any sum you consider fair, provided that at the end of three months that amount will become my salary. The sum I am to pay you can be deducted from what you pay me when I start to earn money.

"General Ayres," Hill recalls, "was so taken with my letter that he hired me." At the end of the first month the famous attorney began paying him a regular salary, and before long the young man was one of his trusted lieutenants.

Legal work appealed to Hill so much that, for a while, he considered making it his career. When he was 18 he decided to matriculate at Georgetown University Law School, in Washington, D.C., in order to qualify for the bar. Doing so required tremendous nerve. He had no money to finance his education. However, he did have an idea. Since he had made money writing for newspapers, he felt that he might do so again. This time he wanted to specialize in writing biographical stories about successful people . . . the kind of stories that many magazines of the period were publishing.

HILL MEETS SUCCESS PERSONIFIED

As a first step he approached Senator Bob Taylor of Tennessee. In addition to being a senator, Taylor was the publisher of an important periodical of the day. Young Hill wanted some assurance of a regular income from his writing. Taylor, intrigued by the young man, offered to give him letters of introduction to prominent people who might make good subjects for future articles. When their interview was over, Hill's list included Thomas Edison; John Wanamaker, the merchant prince; Edward Bok, publisher of the *Ladies' Home Journal*; Cyrus H. K. Curtis, publisher of the *Saturday Evening Post*; Dr. Alexander Graham Bell, inventor of the telephone; and Andrew Carnegie, the great steel magnate.

Dazzled by the prospects of his new connections, Hill put his legal studies aside and threw himself into journalism. The turning point in his life came during his interview with Andrew Carnegie, the man who had built one of the most powerful industrial empires in human history.

After a trip to Pittsburgh, Hill went direct to Carnegie's office. They spent three hours talking about the magnate's life. At the end of that time Carnegie, greatly impressed with the young man, asked him to be a guest in his home. Their talks continued for three days. While he was reviewing the incidents that led to his own rise, Carnegie, once a penniless immigrant in a new land, told Hill that the world needed a philosophy of success based upon the "know-how" of men like himself who had gained their knowledge by experience over a lifetime, by the trial and error method . . . it needed some type of blueprint that would help people make the most of their talents. The job would be long and arduous . . . it would be exhausting . . . and it might not be remunerative for a long time. But someone, he insisted, would have to undertake the task.

At the end of the third day Carnegie suddenly confronted his youthful interlocutor with a question. "Would you," he asked, "be willing to spend 20 years doing the job? Just answer 'yes' or 'no.' Take as much time as you need to make your decision and let me know about it when you do."

THE ANSWER THAT PAID A JACKPOT

Hill, startled, sat back. Moments later the 19-year-old youth blurted out, "Yes, I'll do the job and you may depend on me to complete it!"

Carnegie drew a watch from his hand and showed it to Hill. "It took you 29 seconds to decide. I was giving you 60 seconds to make your mind up!"

Later Hill discovered that the famed industrialist had asked other men if they would undertake the task he suggested . . . but only Hill had met his qualifications.

Thus Napoleon Hill began the monumental task of his life—the organization of his unique philosophy of success . . . a philosophy published, as Carnegie had predicted, more than a score of years later, and subsequently read by millions.

Hill began his work by making intensive studies of the

lives of 500 of the most successful people in the nation, starting with Henry Ford at about the time that the famous Model T automobile made its appearance. Carnegie helped by giving him letters of introduction to top men. Henry Ford, William Wrigley, Jr., and others of similar stature were included.

Although the great men he met were cooperating in supplying information, they did little, if anything, to improve his financial status. During the long years that followed, while he was working on the philosophy of success and testing the "laws" that revealed themselves to him, his life took many turns. It was in this crucible of experience and effort, in the cauldron of success and failure, that *The Law of Success* was born.

His rise was spurred shortly after his marriage in 1910 when he visited his wife's family in Lumberport, West Virginia. The community had long been plagued by the absence of an adequate bridge to carry traffic over the nearby Monongahela River.

The young man, using what he had learned from Carnegie, contacted public officials and business executives. By explaining how all would benefit, he persuaded them to share the costs, then in excess of $100,000. And the town had its long-needed bridge! Moreover, the building of the bridge brought street railway transportation to the town and with it a new surge of business prosperity on which Hill and his wife's relatives were quick to capitalize. A company was organized to produce natural gas, and it became so profitable that it relieved Hill from all financial needs of his family from that time forward, and sent his three sons through the State University. During the 44 years of operations the business has yielded a gross income of many millions of dollars and it is now under the control of Hill's eldest son.

THE TEN RULES OF SUCCESS

When asked how he had done it, Hill explained the 10-point success formula Carnegie had suggested as a starting point for his research:

1. Definiteness of Purpose—the setting of a major goal or purpose.
2. Master-Mind Alliance—contacting and working with people who have what you haven't.
3. Going the Extra Mile—doing more than you have to do is the only thing that justifies raises or promotions, and puts people under an obligation to you.
4. Applied Faith—the kind of belief that has *action* behind it.
5. Personal Initiative—do what you should do without being told to do it.
6. Imagination—daring to do what you think is possible.
7. Enthusiasm—the contagious quality that will attract correlative enthusiasm.
8. Accurate Thinking—the ability to separate facts from fiction and to use those pertinent to your own concerns or problems.
9. Concentration of Effort—not being diverted from any purpose.

10. Profiting by Adversity—remembering that there is an equivalent benefit for every setback.

His success brought national publicity and an offer to direct a leading correspondence school—at a salary and commission reputed to be in excess of the then-fabulous sum of $15,000 per year. In only two years, he brought the firm more than a million dollars in capital and enabled it to multiply its operations. Hill then decided to operate his own school, and spent the next two years teaching advertising. The philosophy of success, then formulating itself in his mind, was tested daily in all he did . . . and it worked.

GOVERNMENT APPLIES SUCCESS FORMULA

At this juncture World War I came. Hill, who had met Woodrow Wilson through Carnegie while the President was head of Princeton University, was asked to come to Washington to serve as a confidential advisor on propaganda to the Chief Executive. His wartime activities did much to stimulate the patriotic fervor required for victory.

When the vast German military machine collapsed in 1918, Hill suggested a plan which helped to destroy the ancient Hohenzollern dynasty and put the Kaiser to flight! President Wilson barely finished reading the request for an armistice when he turned to Hill and showed him the dispatch. "Mr. President," Hill exclaimed, "shouldn't we ask whether this request is made in the name of the German people—or in the name of the Imperial Government?" This question, echoed by Wilson, led to the Kaiser's abdication. It ended the reign of one of the most powerful Royal Houses in the world . . . and stimulated the overthrow of other absolute monarchies.

After Wilson's death and the inauguration of a new administration, Hill decided to return to his work as an educator. He continued to teach and lecture . . . to spread the ideas and the philosophy that he was gleaning from his constant study of the factors that produced success. At one of his lectures he met Don Mellet, publisher of the Canton, Ohio, *Daily News*, who became one of his greatest admirers, and subsequently his manager. Mellet urged Hill to reduce his research to paper . . . and to prepare a manuscript based on his findings, which could be published in book form. As a result, Hill began the actual writing.

Before the work was completed, Mellet was murdered by a policeman and four underworld characters now serving life terms in the Ohio State Penitentiary. Mellet uncovered a tie-in between the four men by which they were permitted to sell narcotics and liquor, and published their names in his paper. The assassination followed and Hill barely missed the same fate, because the underworld characters believed he was behind the newspaper attacks. Before his death Mellet had arranged with Judge Elbert H. Gary, Chairman of the Board of the United States Steel Corporation, to supply the money for the publication of the Hill success books, but Judge Gary died before the deal could be consummated. All in all, the Hand of Destiny, or whatever it is that so often puts men to severe tests before they are permitted to "arrive," seemed to be dealing Hill the losing cards during this dramatic period of his career.

HILL BECOMES A COLUMNIST

After a year he went to Philadelphia to contact Albert L. Pelton, a publisher. Pelton, after glancing at the manuscripts, bought them. Thus the world was given his first major publication—*The Law of Success*—a work subsequently published in eight volumes and now distributed throughout the world.

After the publication of *The Law of Success*, Hill's rise was meteoric. His royalties hit the $2,500 a month mark and stayed at that level for years. Success-starved people everywhere made it their blueprint for a better future.

He traveled constantly . . . lecturing, teaching, and explaining his philosophy. Eventually, Bernard McFadden, the famed publisher, persuaded him to write a daily column for his newspaper—the *Daily Graphic*. The column, called "Success," became one of the publication's principal features and upped the circulation by over 200,000 during the first three months. Eventually, the *Daily Graphic* failed. McFadden jokingly said it was due to Hill's column which built circulation too far ahead of the sale of advertising space. Actually, it was said that the merchants of New York City boycotted the McFadden paper by refusing to give it their advertising, due to some misunderstanding they had with the publisher.

An opportunity for even greater service arrived when Hill's protégé, Jennings Randolph, was elected to Congress. Randolph met Hill when he delivered the commencement address at his graduation from Salem College in West Virginia in 1922. Now assistant to the president of Capital Airlines, a post he took after 14 years in Congress, Randolph had been one of Hill's disciples since his youth. *The Law of Success* had proved its value to him . . . and he, in turn, was eager to assist Hill in giving his talents a wider scope. Through his efforts and those of Steve Early, presidential press secretary, Hill returned to the White House in 1933. The Depression had started and much of Hill's work was devoted to publicizing the NRA, and to efforts designed to restore faith in the government. It was during this period that he contributed the idea that "the only thing we have to fear is fear itself."

MILLIONS LEARN SUCCESS RULES

After the crisis had passed its peak, Hill left the government to return to writing and lecturing on his philosophy from the most important platform in the nation. By 1937 he had completed his second book—*Think and Grow Rich!* One of the most widely read and most profitable books ever published, it is estimated that more than 60,000,000 people throughout the U.S. and more than a score of foreign countries have read it. In the period since its publication Hill estimates that it has produced approximately $23,000,000 in revenue.

Hill bought an estate in Florida and retired. But he was too full of ideas . . . too urgently needed to remain in isolation. By 1940 he had had enough of inactivity and he returned to the work which had given substance to his life . . . the propagation of the philosophy of success that his endless researches had produced.

The circumstances that brought him back to public activity were typical. He recalls, "Mark Wooding, a student of mine, had just opened a restaurant in Atlanta, Georgia, and I learned that he was in financial difficulties. I could not forget the many times my friend had come to my rescue when I needed help so I took a plane and flew to Atlanta to see what I could do to assist him."

Hill rescued his friends by giving a series of lectures on his success philosophy to evening diners. Their ticket of admission was their dinner check. Business boomed as word of Hill's lectures spread.

During the course of these lectures, he met Dr. William P. Jacobs, president of Presbyterian College at Clinton, South Carolina. The college president, who operated a large printing establishment in addition to his other interests, urged Hill to rewrite his entire philosophy of personal achievement, and offered to publish it in a new edition.

On the first day of January, 1941, Hill began transcribing the shorthand notes he had taken during his many conferences with Andrew Carnegie, and by the end of the year—one day before Pearl Harbor—the job was finished.

The result was the publication of his 16-volume work—
Mental Dynamite!

After the appearance of the first edition, the war-born paper shortage forced a halt to the project. Yet Hill takes pride in the chain of events that led to the publication of this work. "It illustrates," he says, "the value of lending a helping hand—the power produced by 'going the extra mile.' I didn't have to help my friend Wooding make his restaurant a success. But, because I did, I also reaped a benefit!"

YOU CAN, IF YOU WILL

He used this illustration, among many others in his personal experience, to prove the validity of his theory of "Cosmic Habit-Force." This theory is based on the idea that "Whatever the mind can conceive and believe, the mind can achieve." In other words, if you are convinced you can do something, you will ultimately be able to do it, despite any obstacles that may exist. He believed that he could help his friend and he did—and out of that service the "law of compensation" more than repaid him for his efforts.

During the war Hill gave his services to industry—assisting in eliminating potential sources of labor friction in important plants. And, in 1944, feeling that he was ready to go into semi-retirement, he and his wife moved to California. On his arrival in Los Angeles he found that his books and his philosophy were being read and used by countless thousands. Los Angeles' chief library had 71 well-thumbed copies of *Think and Grow Rich!* It led all books in its field.

Because of his tremendous West Coast following, Hill became a radio commentator and his program over KFWB, in Los Angeles, during the next three years, was one of the most popular ever produced in that area.

But a new and probably the most important phase of his life was still ahead of him. It began in 1951 when, at the request of one of his former students, he went to St. Louis to conduct a training program based on his success philosophy for a group of 350 men. While teaching this group he met a dentist who invited him to deliver an address before a group of 50 dentists in Chicago. Hill accepted the invitation.

BEGINS NEW CAREER

It was a fateful decision. As has been true throughout his long and productive life, his eagerness to serve others gave him still greater opportunities. One of the guests at the meeting was W. Clement Stone, Jr., who had been invited by his dentist to hear Hill speak. Young Stone, the son of one of the nation's leading insurance executives, hastened to introduce himself when Hill arrived.

"My father," he told the success scientist, "has been a life-long student of your philosophy. In fact, he built his multi-million-dollar business on the basis of the principles described in your books."

Hill, telling of the meeting, says, "When he told me that his father was president of the Combined Insurance Company of America I recalled that the firm had, from time to time through the years, purchased large quantities of practically all my books."

At the luncheon intermission, Hill was introduced to W. Clement Stone, Sr., who, he learned, had canceled airplane passage for an important business trip to hear his talk. Stone went on to tell him how much *The Law of Success*, *Think and Grow Rich*, *Mental Dynamite*, and other Hill publications had done for him . . . and he catapulted a new idea. "Your success philosophy should be recorded in motion pictures that thousands can see and hear. It should be presented in a form that can do the greatest number the greatest good!"

Then the multi-millionaire insurance magnate went on to offer his services in furthering this project if Hill would agree to it. Exhilarated by this new idea, Hill studied the proposal and, ultimately, accepted. Later, his alliance with Stone was broadened to make the executive his general manager. Under the terms of the contract they agreed upon, he became Hill's exclusive manager and publisher. As a result, a new organization was developed—Napoleon Hill Associates. Through this group the principals hope to multiply Hill's ability to reach the countless millions who need his help. They hope to give more men the remarkable success formula that has done so much for others who have studied its precepts and applied them.

The alliance between Stone and Hill has already borne much fruit. It has resulted in the publication of *How to Raise Your Own Salary*, in the preparation of a new manuscript to be published under the title *How to Find Peace of Mind*, in the filming of motion pictures which preserve Hill's dy-

namic personality and verbatim precepts for future generations, and in the creation of a corps of men and women
who are studying directly under Hill with a view to being
teachers of his doctrine. They will ultimately multiply his
own person by simultaneously teaching the Hill philosophy
in cities, towns, and villages throughout the country.

REVITALIZES ALL

That the philosophy works goes without saying. Paris, Missouri, is a typical example. Hill taught one group in that
small Midwestern town how to use and apply his precepts.
Within a year the town, a sleepy little hamlet which had
changed little since Civil War days, was completely revitalized. Today new buildings, a new church, and many civic
improvements have altered it completely. And a continu-
ous program of further improvement is in store. Hill's graduates, permanently banded together in a group they call
"Club Success Unlimited," continue to work for further advances.

Today Hill and Stone, working together, look forward
to the day when "Success Unlimited" will be the watch-
words of all . . . when every man and every woman who
wants more out of life . . . when all who are concerned with
creating a better future will be linked together in similar
groups.

To make this possible for everyone . . . even those whose
homes are in isolated and remote areas, they have developed

home study programs, plans for individual study groups, and special classes to be conducted under the direction of specially trained teachers and moderators. And they plan to accomplish during the next 5 years that which would ordinarily require 50 years of planning and labor, including the translation of the Science of Success into the leading languages of the world.

BASIC PRINCIPLES PROVIDE SUCCESS

Hill's philosophy remains a living, growing concept of men and the factors that govern their lives. Over the years it has expanded In addition to the 10 basic principles he obtained from Carnegie, men like Ford, Edison, and almost 500 other leaders who collaborated in his search for the ingredients of individual success contributed 7 additional points. They are:

1. The Golden Rule Applied—sowing the seeds one is willing to harvest.
2. Cosmic Habit-Force—the controlling law of Nature through which all habits are formed, described abstractly in Emerson's Law of Compensation.
3. Concentration—sticking to a task until it has been completed or discarded for sufficient cause.
4. Pleasing Personality—a trait that can be developed and constantly improved.
5. Self-Control—mastery over thoughts, speech, and deeds.

6. Habit of Health—temperance in eating, exercising, thinking, and drinking.
7. Habit of Saving—budgeting time, income, and expenditures.

The formula appears to be simple . . . it appears to be basic. Yet, it represents the distilled effort of a lifetime. Relatively few men in the history of the world have been able to apply all of the principles at all times. Hill, the man who has already taught millions how to succeed, hopes to teach still more how they can master these essentials of success. If he does, he is certain that the power this knowledge will give men . . . this key to individual success . . . can be an effective antidote for the kind of frustration and discontent that produces wars . . . that converts failures to communism.

"If you have the power to advance . . . if you are certain that you can have a better future, you'll never surrender your birthright of freedom," he exclaims.

From *Salesman's Opportunity: The Magazine of Successful Selling*, November, 1954

FAITH IS THE MASTER KEY
TO THE SCIENCE OF SUCCESS

by Napoleon Hill

If ye have faith as a grain of mustard seed, ye shall say unto this mountain, Remove hence to yonder place; and it shall remove; and nothing shall be impossible unto you (Matthew 17:20).

Faith is the Master Key with which we may unlock the door that separates our earthly destinies from the universe's eternal source of power. Science has unlocked the secret of the power of the atom, mastered the skies above us and the oceans beneath us, and revealed to us vehicles of transportation that move faster than sound, but science has not explained the inexorable power of faith.

I think I know something about the subject of applied faith, and I know it, not from theory and not from reading a book, but from actual observation and experience.

Let me tell you how I came face to face with my first big opportunity to test my faith when I was just a young man.

I had just finished a three-day interview with Andrew Carnegie, philanthropist and founder of the United S

Steel Corporation. Mr. Carnegie at that time was the richest man in the world. He had commissioned me to become the author of the world's first practical philosophy of personal achievement, but he loaded the assignment with the condition that I would have to devote 20 years to research and earn my own living as I went along, without a financial subsidy from him.

I tried desperately to decline the assignment on the grounds that I did not have the necessary finances to support me through 20 years of profitless labor; I did not have sufficient education to justify me in undertaking such an assignment; and, worse still, I was not sure I understood the meaning of the word "philosophy."

All of those "alibis" sprang into my mind while I sat there in Mr. Carnegie's library as he waited for my answer, but somehow, I could not open my mouth to decline the wonderful opportunity he had given me. Then, like a flash of lightning, a great light came over me, and the room seemed as if a floodlight had been turned upon it. And something inside me said, "Tell him you will accept the assignment." And I did!

When I reported to my relatives that I had accepted a 20-year job without pay and they discovered that my employer was the richest man in the world, they made it plain that they believed I had lost my mind.

But I was happy because I realized I had met successfully my first big opportunity to move on my own capacity for faith.

During my 20 years of labor with Mr. Carnegie I learned many things. One profound fact I discovered was that every adversity, every failure, every defeat, and every unpleasant circumstance of our lives brings with it the seed of an equivalent benefit. *The Creator has wisely provided that nothing of value can be taken from anyone without something of equal or greater value being made available to take its place.*

Search wherever you may, you will never find a more profound truth than this—a truth that will give you consolation and lead you out of the depths of despair when you are overtaken by grief—*provided you move on faith.*

During the years of research and organization of the Science of Success, I was overtaken by no less than 20 major defeats, each of which provided me with a glorious opportunity to test my capacity for faith. Had it not been for the knowledge revealed to me by these defeats, the Science of Success philosophy could not have been completed during my lifetime.

Perhaps the greatest blessing that came to me through my experiences with defeat was the revelation that prayer can give us guidance, but to benefit by it, we must do something on our own account. Also, the most effective of all our prayers are those which we offer as an expression of gratitude for the blessings we already enjoy, rather than asking for more blessings.

After I learned to pray in this way, my blessings began to multiply, until at long last I had everything I desired or needed without having to ask for more. An important turning point in my life was reached the day I first said, "Oh, Lord, I ask not for more blessings, but for more wisdom with which to make better use of the blessings you gave me at birth—the privilege of controlling and directing my own mind to purposes of my choice."

The mind is so designed that it attracts the sum and substance of what one thinks about most often. As a matter of fact, life brings everyone that which his mind dwells upon, whether his thoughts are based on fear or faith. The majority of people go through life with their mindpower directed by fears and self-imposed limitations, and they wonder why life is so unkind to them.

Fear is nothing but faith in reverse gear! The foundation on which both faith and fear rests is belief in something.

Another thing I learned while working with Mr. Carnegie was that if you make the best possible use of whatever tools or circumstances that come into your possession with the faith that you will attain your desires, better tools and circumstances will be mysteriously revealed to you. If you have a purpose in mind which you desire to attain, the place to begin is right where you stand.

The only qualification I had for accepting Andrew Carnegie's commission to organize the Science of Success was an unshakable faith that the ways and means of successfully carrying out the mission would be revealed to me as I went along. And they always were!

Here is something that will show you how mysteriously the Lord works. I recognized long ago that I had to have an automatic system for taking care of all my needs. I adopted what I call my Nine Invisible Guides. I call them my Nine Princes.

My system of Applied Faith consists of nine invisible entities which I was inspired to create in my mind. Each of them draws upon and uses the stock of *faith credits* which I have accumulated by expressing gratitude for the blessings I desire even before I receive them. I don't know if these guides are imaginary or not. Maybe the Lord has really set them up as invisible effigies; but they are just as effective as if they were real.

The Prince of Sound Health works while I sleep to keep my physical body healed and in normal working condition for the housing and administration of my mind. Every cell of my body is revitalized with the energy necessary to give it efficiency in functioning.

The Prince of Financial Prosperity attends to my every financial need by inspiring me to render useful service in proportion to my financial requirements. Although I was born in poverty and lived in poverty during my childhood, my financial needs no longer give me any concern whatso-ever. They are automatically supplied, giving me freedom from money worries.

The Prince of Peace of Mind keeps my mind eternally free from the causes of fear and worry, thus conditioning it for the expression of faith.

The Princes of Hope and Faith are twins. They work to-gether to keep me active with duties which enrich my own life and help me to enrich the lives of others, through the books I write and the personal counsel I am privileged to offer many of my friends. And they help me to see a successful ending to every undertaking, even before I begin a given objective. Of more importance, hope and faith together serve as the Master Key by which I may open the door to Infinite Intelligence at will for any purpose I desire.

The Princes of Love and Romance are also twins. They keep me youthful in both mind and body, and clothe all of my activities with a spirit of love, which makes them a powerful influence for the benefit of all whom they serve.

The Prince of Patience gives me a well-balanced life and helps me to time my thoughts and deeds through self-discipline so they are effective and beneficial to all whom they influence. And this prince helps me to relate myself to others in a spirit of understanding and tolerance, which makes for enduring friendships.

The Prince of Overall Wisdom so relates me to all the influences which touch my life—past, present and future—that I benefit from each of them, whether they are pleasant or unpleasant. And this prince also guides me in the right direction when I reach the crossroads of life where I must make decisions beyond the scope of my education, experience and native ability.

In addition, my faith is a sort of roving ambassador whose duty it is to run errands and render general service which has not been assigned to the nine guides.

Sometimes faith is called upon to perform service for

me which cannot be classified as of minor importance. For example, several years ago my wife and I decided to sell our home in California and move back to Greenville, South Carolina, in order that I might save time commuting by airplane between my home and my office in Chicago, Illinois.

We had very definite ideas as to the sort of house and location we desired. First of all, it had to be located in a first-class neighborhood. It had to be on a large plot of ground, well-stocked with a great variety of trees. The house had to be of the rambling type that would permit the addition of more rooms if we desired them, and it had to be located on a well-balanced, sloping hill. Last, but not of the least importance, it had to be within a certain price range. This was not an easy combination of requirements to be found in Greenville, or elsewhere, for that matter.

But we confidently put faith to work, and within a matter of days, we were led to the precise spot that met our every requirement.

In our home we express no negative words, give room to no negative thoughts, but surcharge the entire premises with hope and faith and love and romance. Each day we bless every room in our home. We bless our entire forest of beautiful trees and flowers. We bless the neighbors whose properties touch ours. We bless the songbirds that feed at our "bird cafeteria" and bathe in our birdbath. And we bless our multitudinous friends throughout the world, although we have seen but few of them in person.

Lastly, we bless you as you read this message, and sincerely hope you may find in it some expression that will enrich your own life and give it greater power for good in all your human relations.

From *The Cadle Call*, April 1964, Vol. XXIII, No. 9, pp. 8–10

CAUGHT ON THE WING:
"GOING THE EXTRA MILE"
PAYS, NAPOLEON HILL SAYS

by Charles H. Garrison

Today's guest artist is Napoleon Hill, a nationally known writer
and lecturer, who is now making his home at Clinton. Mr. Hill
is a native of southwestern Virginia, a former banker who
something like 30 years ago was selected by Andrew Carnegie,
from a multitude of applicants, for the important task of analyzing business methods of some of America's industrial giants.
From that beginning Mr. Hill has continued until his methods
are known and used in many foreign countries, as well as in
America. His article for today is "Going the Extra Mile," and
has a practical, everyday appeal for those who read it.

O ver 30 years ago Andrew Carnegie held a stop-
watch, hidden under his desk while he counted
the reaction time required for me to recognize
and embrace an opportunity he offered me. The opportunity consisted of the privilege of organizing the Philosophy

of American Achievement, based on the experiences of Mr. Carnegie, Thomas A. Edison, Henry Ford, John Wanamaker, Cyrus H. K. Curtis, Dr. Alexander Graham Bell, and others of achievement under the American way of life.

Through the research the 17 principles of individual achievement were uncovered, the most useful one of which is probably the habit of Going the Extra Mile!

I chose the principle of Going the Extra Mile for analysis in this column today for the reason that the whole world is rapidly becoming spiritually bankrupt mainly because a majority of the people have put this principle in reverse gear by trying to get something for nothing! I suspect it is because the real spiritual meaning of the rule has not been generally understood. In final analysis it is the Golden Rule streamlined and applied to human relationships in all walks of life. Lloyd Douglas caught the full meaning of this great universal rule and interpreted it in his book, *Magnificent Obsession*, which made a profound impression on those who read the book.

This country may need a two-ocean navy; it may need the largest fleet of airplanes in the world; it may need production of war materials on a huge scale; and I think it needs all these; but what it needs most of all is for the people, all of us, to stop trying to get without giving, and begin now, to Go the Extra Mile, in the same spirit that the 56 men who signed the Declaration of Independence applied this rule, when the "freest and richest" country known to civilization was born.

This is not only the way to salvation of our souls (for

some of us seem not so much concerned about our souls as we are about our pocketbooks) but it is the quickest and surest way to self-determination economically, for it is as true as that night follows day, that the man who does more than he is paid for, and does it in a pleasant mental attitude, sooner or later is paid for more than he does. The rule has never been known to fail during the thirty-odd years I have been observing it.

Take my own experience for example: Andrew Carnegie said, "If you will Go the Extra Mile and put 20 years of unpaid labor into finding out what helps me to get ahead and stay ahead, you will not only confer a lasting benefit on millions yet unborn, but the results of your labor will give you economic security the remainder of your life, if you never do another thing."

MEET DR. JACOBS

I believed what he said, for he had demonstrated in his own life that he knew the rules of individual achievement, one of which—Going the Extra Mile—he applied so successfully that his huge fortune still goes marching on, helping to educate people who wish to get ahead by their own efforts instead of trying to get something for nothing. I have been rewarded beyond my fondest hopes, for today the Philosophy of American Achievement has become known around the world, and Dr. William Plumer Jacobs, president of Presbyterian College, and I are publishing it in a popular edition for the use of the masses in this country, under a plan which we hope will enable us to offset the spread of the now popular habit of trying to get something for nothing.

It had been my hope, for years, to present this philosophy to the American people (in fulfillment of my promise to Mr. Carnegie) at the bare cost of rendering the service, but my difficulty was in finding a publisher who had enough vision to adopt the principle of Going the Extra Mile and think in terms of serving the people instead of earning dividends.

I finally found the right man when, by a series of unusual circumstances I was privileged to meet Dr. Jacobs. I had been looking for a publisher among the great publishing houses of the East, but I found him in the little town of Clinton, South Carolina, the last place on earth I would have gone in search of someone with enough creative vision to help me render the people of America such a service as the one we have undertaken to render.

TO AID YOUTHS

Despite all his business responsibilities, Dr. Jacobs has helped me re-write, entirely, the Philosophy of American Achievement. He went at this job with enthusiasm such as I had never before witnessed, for he saw in the philosophy a means of setting the youth of America (as well as the adults) straight in their thinking, and this is a job that must be done, and done now, if the American way of life is to endure for the next generation. We have worked out a plan for teaching this philosophy to the 500,000 young men and young women who graduate in the business colleges annually; these who will become the business and industrial leaders of tomorrow. We also have a plan for teaching it to the high school graduates and those who go on to college.

This is the type of service which we shall perform without the thought of commercial profit, for we realize that the huge debt that this generation is piling up for the next and succeeding generations is so great—a debt that consists of much more than money—that it will destroy the American way of life unless the people put aside greed and selfishness and come back, once more, to that simple rule of life laid down by the Nazarene, in the Sermon on the Mount; a rule which we have streamlined and embodied in the principle of Going the Extra Mile.

PRACTICE IS BEST

The best way, Dr. Jacobs believes, to teach any rule is by practicing it! That is why he has thrown himself into the job of helping to spread the Philosophy of American Achievement, although it may become a huge draft upon his time and energies. He believes that the youths of America are entitled to a "break" from the people of this generation who are piling up obligations for the future, and he is demonstrating his belief by action, not words.

We are living in a world that is sick, but there is nothing wrong with it that could not be cured, overnight, if the people stopped trying to get something for nothing and began Going the Extra Mile, in the spirit recommended by the greatest of all philosophers. The unfortunate people of France found this out, but not soon enough. Let us profit by their failure, not by trying to outdo each other in getting but by heeding the admonition to the philosopher who said, "Help thy brother's boat across and lo! thine own hath reached the shore."

From *Greenville Piedmont*, August 5, 1941

GET READY TO SUCCEED! HEALTH, HAPPINESS, AND WEALTH CAN BE YOURS—IF YOU KNOW WHAT YOU WANT

by Napoleon Hill and W. Clement Stone

Meet the most important living person! Somewhere in this article you may meet him—suddenly, surprisingly, and with a shock of recognition that will change your whole life. When you do meet him, you will discover his secret. You will discover that he carries with him an invisible talisman with the initials PMA emblazoned on one side, and NMA on the other.

This invisible talisman has two amazing powers: It has the power to attract wealth, success, happiness, and health; and it has the power to repel these things—to rob you of all that makes life worth living. It is the first of these powers, PMA, that enables some men to climb to the top and stay there. It is the second that keeps other men at the bottom all their lives. It is NMA that pulls other men down from the top when they have reached it.

Perhaps the story of S. B. Fuller will illustrate:

"We are poor—not because of God." S. B. Fuller was one of seven children of a tenant farmer in Louisiana. By the time he was nine, he was driving mules. These families accepted poverty as their lot.

Young Fuller was blessed in the midst of poverty in one way: He had a remarkable mother. She used to talk to her son about her dreams. "We shouldn't be poor," she used to say. "And don't ever let me hear you say that it is God's will that we are poor. We are poor—not because of God. We are poor because father has never developed a desire to become rich. No one in our family has ever developed a desire to be anything else."

No one had developed a *desire* to be wealthy. This idea became so deeply ingrained in Fuller's mind that it changed his whole life. He began to *want* to be rich. The quickest way to make money, he decided, was to sell something. He chose soap. For 12 years he sold it, door to door. Then he learned that the company which supplied him was going to be sold at auction. The firm price was $150,000. In 12 years he had saved $25,000. It was agreed that he would deposit his $25,000 and obtain the balance within 10 days. If he did not raise the money, he would lose his deposit.

During his 12 years as a soap salesman, S. B. Fuller had gained the respect and admiration of many business men. He went to them now. He obtained money from personal friends, too, and from loan companies and investment groups. On the eve of the 10th day, he had raised $115,000. He was $10,000 short.

Search for the light. "I had exhausted every source of credit I knew," he recalls. "It was late at night. In the darkness of my room I knelt down and prayed. I asked God to lead me to a person who would let me have the $10,000 in time. I said to myself that I would drive down 61st Street until I saw the first light in a business establishment. I asked God to make the light a sign indicating His answer."

It was 11 o'clock when S. B. Fuller drove down Chicago's 61st Street. At last, after several blocks, he saw a light in a contractor's office.

He walked in. There, seated at his desk, tired from working late at night, sat a man whom Fuller knew slightly. Fuller realized that he would have to be bold. "Do you want to make $1,000?" asked Fuller.

The contractor was taken aback. "Yes," he said. "Of course." "Then make out a check for $10,000 and when I bring back the money, I'll bring back $1,000 profit," Fuller recalls telling this man. He gave the contractor the names of the other people who had lent him money, and explained in detail exactly what the business venture was.

Let's explore his secret of success. Before he left that night, S. B. Fuller had a check for $10,000 in his pocket. Today he owns controlling interest not only in that company, but in seven others, including four cosmetic companies, a hosiery company, a label company, and a newspaper. When we asked him recently to explore with us the secret of his success, he answered in terms of his mother's statement so many years before:

"We are poor—not because of God. We are poor because father has never developed a desire to become rich. No one in our family has ever developed a desire to be anything else."

"You see," he told us, "I knew what I wanted, but I didn't know how to get it. So I read the Bible and inspirational books. I prayed for the knowledge to achieve my objectives. If you know what you want, you are more apt to recognize it when you see it."

S. B. Fuller carried with him the invisible talisman with the initials PMA imprinted on one side and NMA on the other. He turned the PMA side up and amazing things happened. He was able to bring into reality ideas that were formerly mere day dreams.

In these times and in this country you still have your personal right to say: "This is what I choose. This is what I want most to accomplish." And unless your goal is against the laws of God or society, you can achieve it.

What you try for is up to you. Not everyone would care to be an S. B. Fuller, responsible for large manufacturing concerns. Not everyone would choose to pay the costly price of being a great artist. But whether success to you means becoming rich, or the discovery of a new element in chemistry, or the creation of a piece of music, or the growing of a rose, or the nurturing of a child, the invisible talisman can help you achieve it.

Take the story of Clem Labine. He is best known throughout the baseball world as a pitcher who could throw one of the best curves in the game: a jug-handled curve.

When Clem was a boy, he broke the index finger on his

right hand. It healed, but there was a permanent crook between the first and second joints. It seemed to Clem that this was the end of his dream of a baseball career.

Every adversity has the seed of a greater benefit. "Don't be so sure," his coach told him. "Sometimes the things that seem like disasters turn out to be blessings in disguise. It is said that *every adversity has the seed of a greater benefit.*"

Clem took the advice to heart. Soon he discovered that he had a natural pitching arm and that the crooked finger could be put to good use. The bend gave the ball a twist and a spin that no other pitcher on his team possessed. Year after year he worked to develop this spin until he became one of the really fine pitchers of our day.

How did he accomplish this? Through natural skill, hard work, and—even more important—through a change in mental attitude. Clem Labine had learned to look for the good in his unfortunate situation. He used his invisible talisman, turning up the PMA side. He attracted success to himself with PMA.

A man of 25 has before him some 100,000 working hours should he retire at 65. How many of your working hours will be alive with the magnificent force of PMA? And how many of them will have the life knocked out of them with the stunning blows of NMA?

Meet the most important living person. The day you recognize PMA for yourself is the day that you will meet the most important living person! Who is he? Why, the most important living person is *you*, as far as you and your life are concerned. Take a look at yourself. Isn't it true that you carry with you an invisible talisman with the initials PMA emblazoned on one side and NMA on the other? The talisman is your mind. PMA is Positive Mental Attitude.

A Positive Mental Attitude is most often comprised of the "plus" characteristics symbolized by such words as faith, integrity, hope, optimism, courage, initiative, generosity, tolerance, tact, kindliness, and good common sense.

NMA is a negative mental attitude. It has opposite characteristics. These are powerful forces. Your success, health, happiness, and wealth depend on how you use your invisible talisman.

Think of it! Think of the people who drift aimlessly through life, dissatisfied, struggling *against* a great many things, but without a clear-cut goal. Can you state, right now, what it is that you want out of life? Fixing your goals may not be easy. It may even involve some painful self-examination. But it will be worth whatever effort it costs, because as soon as you can name your goal, you can expect to enjoy many advantages. These advantages come almost automatically.

1. The first great advantage is that your subconscious mind begins to work under a universal law: "What the mind can *conceive* and *believe*—the mind can *achieve*." Because you visualize your intended destination, your subconscious mind is affected by this self-suggestion. It goes to work to help you get there.
2. Because you know what you want, there is a tendency for you to try to get on the right track and head in the right direction. You get into action.

3. Work now becomes fun. You are motivated to pay the price. You budget your time and money. You study, think, and plan. The more you think about your goals, the more enthusiastic you become. And with enthusiasm your desire turns into a *burning* desire.

4. You become alerted to opportunities that will help you achieve your objectives as they present themselves in your everyday experiences. Because you know what you want, you are more likely to recognize these opportunities.

When you have a Positive Mental Attitude, the problems of your world tend to bow before you. The payoff is success, health, happiness, wealth.

From *Chicago Sunday Tribune Magazine*, June 19, 1960, pp. 37 and 39

MR. CARNEGIE'S PROTÉGÉ CLAIMS HE'S . . . THE MAN WHO'S HELPED MILLIONS TO MAKE MILLIONS

by Ray Castle

Modesty obviously is not one of the 17 principles of the "Science of Success" which has enabled Dr. Napoleon Hill to accumulate a vast fortune.

Because Dr. Hill admits that, as well as making himself a millionaire, he has helped millions of others to become millionaires, too.

Not a bad record, eh?

After a talk with Dr. Nap I wasn't much farther along the road to making my first million.

Nonetheless, Dr. Hill, an American who claims to have made his first million dollars before he was 21, is here to spread his success philosophy.

Last night he gave a few clues to members of the Sydney

Vizor Club, which, as the name implies, is a group sort of recalling the grand old days of chivalry.

Firstly, how did he get the name Napoleon?

HOPEFUL PARENTS

Hopeful parents named him after a multi-millionaire uncle, trusting the compliment would earn him consideration in the will. But he inherited only the name from his uncle.

"But," said Napoleon in the classically modest statement I outlined above, "I feel I've gone farther than my uncle. For not only have I made money for myself but I've helped millions of others to become millionaires, too."

How?

Well, it seems that as a newspaper scribe at the age of 19 he met the rich industrialist Andrew Carnegie who, in 1908, assigned him to write a philosophy based on his own principles of success in piling up the lucre.

Carnegie paid the young Hill's expenses over the next 20 years as he interviewed people like Henry Ford, Theodore Roosevelt, Elbert Hubbard, Luther Burbank, Woodrow Wilson, Dr. Frank Crane and nearly 500 other giants of the times to prove the philosophy by their own experiences.

The enterprising Nap, meanwhile, employing these success principles, built his brother's natural gas company into a million-dollar concern.

And his eight-volume *Law of Success* was a big hit when published in 1928.

Since then Dr. Hill has published six books, the best known being *Think and Grow Rich.*

In case the title might be too provocative for lethargic types he's bringing out one for lazy bones: *Sleep and Grow Rich.*

All this might sound droll, but it's the story of how Dr. Hill built up a private corporation grossing 120,000 pounds a year.

The Hill "Doctor" handle derives from two honorary degrees conferred on him in the U.S.—for literature and philosophy.

The Hill secret of keeping on top of things: intensive activity; no doctors or drugs; simple living and simple foods. And not too much of them, either.

A final modest touch from this 77-year-old human dynamo: "I could challenge any young man to a sprint three times around the block.

"I'd arrive as calm as anything, while his tongue would be hanging out."

From *The Daily Telegraph*, March 22, 1960

AUTHOR, FORMER ADVISOR
TO PRESIDENTS, TO SPEAK

by T. H. Helgeson

A t 82, Dr. Napoleon Hill leans forward eagerly when he speaks, peering straight ahead and into your eyes and talks of his work passionately like a man of 25.

And for Dr. Hill, though he terms this phase of his life the "afternoon of my·days," life is a pulsating and engrossing matter.

The author of numerous books, including one, *Think and Grow Rich*, which has had millions of readers throughout the world, a presidential advisor to two Presidents of the United States and confidant to some of the greatest men of this century, he has built his life around 13 words: "What the human mind can conceive and believe, the human mind can achieve." This is the core of Dr. Hill's Philosophy; a philosophy, he claims, that represents the fruits of experience acquired by the leading men of this century.

A "success story" himself, Dr. Hill was born in a one-room log cabin in southwest Virginia and was 12 years old before he owned a pair of shoes.

A newspaper reporter in his early youth while attending law school at Georgetown University in Washington, D.C., Dr. Hill began a unique and consuming adventure in 1908, one which would bring him a fortune and place him in intimate contact with more than 500 of the world's most affluent and productive men.

He had been commissioned to write a series of success stories for a magazine and his first assignment was to interview steel magnate Andrew Carnegie.

CARNEGIE INTERVIEW

A three-hour interview with Carnegie was prolonged into one lasting three days and nights. The magnate thrilled and enticed the young reporter with the idea of organizing a philosophy around the principles of success Carnegie himself had employed to acquire his famous millions.

At the conclusion of the grueling interview, Carnegie asked Hill if he was prepared to devote 20 years of his life to unearth and define the motivating forces and underlying factors which determine individual success. Twenty-nine seconds after Carnegie asked, Dr. Hill agreed.

Dr. Hill later learned that Carnegie would have withdrawn the offer if he had deliberated another 31 seconds.

As the years went by, Dr. Hill talked extensively with such men as Carnegie, Thomas A. Edison, Henry Ford, James J. Hill, Theodore Roosevelt, William Jennings Bryan,

John D. Rockefeller, F. W. Woolworth, Clarence Darrow, Woodrow Wilson, Luther Burbank, Alexander Graham Bell, and a myriad of other dynamic personalities who had "made their success."

During an interview Sunday, Dr. Hill said of the principles the renowned figures had in common, the "musts" were "decisiveness of purpose" and the "Master-Mind principle."

The "Master Mind," Dr. Hill describes in *Think and Grow Rich*, is "coordination of knowledge and effort, in a spirit of harmony, between two or more people, for the attainment of a definite purpose." Basically, "Master Mind" is simple utilization of inherent human resources.

Dr. Hill was intrigued with Edison, the great and indefatigable inventor. He tells of how, during their interview, Edison revealed a diary of failures he kept of various aborted inventions that rose high over both their heads.

Edison said to him, "You know I had to succeed, because I ran out of things that didn't work."

FDR, WILSON

Dr. Hill was an advisor to Presidents Woodrow Wilson and Franklin Delano Roosevelt and coined the phrase "We have nothing to fear but fear itself," which became the byword of the Roosevelt administration.

It was at Dr. Hill's suggestion, that FDR commenced his highly successful "fireside chats" during World War II.

Dr. Hill's life, a life he says has been "meteoric," has also been punctuated by the unusual.

In 1909, while still a cub reporter, he became the first "layman" in history to fly when he boarded a plane built by the Wright brothers and flown by Orville Wright.

Dr. Hill said he was with a group of newspaper men dispatched to cover one of the Wrights' history-making flights. The brothers were negotiating the sale of one of their planes to the United States Navy. Stipulations for a pre-sale agreement demanded the plane be flown to Washington, D.C., and that one passenger be aboard.

PASSENGER

Dr. Hill was selected as the passenger, he says, because he was the lightest man in the group. "When we landed," he related, "I had to lift my feet, which were dangling from the bottom of the plane, so they wouldn't drag when we landed."

The Wright brothers, he contends, would have been startled by recent aviation successes.

"They just wanted a machine that could fly a little way and maybe carry two or three passengers."

Dr. Hill's current interest is disseminating the credos of his philosophy in prisons, and it is there, among the "forgotten and hopeless," that he believes his greatest challenge lies. He calls this work his "ministry."

"Life itself," he said, "is a matter of getting lives balanced." "Anyone," he asserts, "can be successful." And success "is being able to get from life everything you desire without infringing upon the rights of other people."

In recent years, Dr. Hill has been involved to a great extent with a non-profit educational undertaking called the Napoleon Hill Foundation.

Through the foundation, he and his associates disseminate the ideas underlying Dr. Hill's accumulated "think and grow rich" philosophy.

Most of Dr. Hill's writing is done at his mountaintop home on Ferris Mountain in South Carolina. His latest book, *Grow Rich With Peace of Mind*, will be published this fall.

Asked to describe his own success story, Dr. Hill said simply, but definitively, "I've learned to make my mind receptive to ideas."

From *Dixon Evening Telegraph*, Monday,
May 2, 1966, p. 11

Part Two

MIAMI DAILY NEWS
SCIENCE OF
SUCCESS SERIES,
JUNE AND JULY 1956

by Napoleon Hill

"Gratitude is a beautiful word. It is beautiful because it describes a state of mind that is deeply spiritual in nature. It enhances one's personality with magnetic charm, and it is the master key that opens the door to the magic powers and the beauty of Infinite Intelligence."

COURTESY HELPS
WIN LEADERSHIP

Courtesy is perhaps the singlemost trait by which Man identifies himself as a civilized being. Indeed, it's the everyday sign of his humanity.

The animal has no consideration for his fellows. Neither, for that matter, did Man in his primitive state. One of the first signs of dawning civilization came when men began establishing standards of conduct between themselves.

By like token, the higher the civilization, the greater degree of courtesy, politeness and consideration its members show for each other. Consider, for example, the elaborate demonstrations of courtesy exchanged in such ancient cultures as the Chinese, the Roman, or the Japanese.

Courtesy is the outward sign of a person's attitude toward other people.

Through it, you can demonstrate your obedience to the commandment—"that ye love one another." And with it, you show the respect, esteem and appreciation you hold for those with whom you come in contact.

SHOW RESPECT FOR SELF

More important, you demonstrate your respect for yourself. Politeness is the ritual by which courtesy is expressed. Its standards and modes—the bowing and curtsying and hat tipping—vary from year to year and from country to country.

STANDARDS DON'T CHANGE

But the standards of courtesy itself never change. They are constant and unfailing.

What has all this to do with you and your dreams of success? Through courtesy, you demonstrate your level of civilization and culture. Only the most advanced, the most civilized and cultured persons, have a right to consider themselves qualified to lead others.

Politeness and courtesy—far from being a mark of servility—show that you have thoughtfulness and concern for the high value and worthwhileness of every person you meet.

SCHWAB AN EXAMPLE

Andrew Carnegie was once asked how Charles M. Schwab happened to become his right hand man, at a huge salary.

"In the first place," Carnegie replied, "it didn't just happen. Charlie made it happen by his limitless capacity to win people over to his way of thinking through unfailing courtesy and tactfulness."

Tactfulness and courtesy are so intertwined that we shall make it the next subject for discussion in our Science of Success series.

Meanwhile, begin today to make courtesy the hallmark of your character.

It will stamp you as a person headed for success—and certain that he's going to achieve it.

TACT HELPS YOU
TO REACH GOAL

Tactfulness is the art of overcoming opposition. Through it you can turn obstacles into stepping-stones to success. Tact requires thoughtfulness, good judgment and the ability to think your way to swift decisions "on your feet," so to speak.

With 'its help, you can say things the way other people want them said and do things the way they want them done.

Notice, please, this doesn't mean that you say what others want to hear or do the things they want you to do. There's considerable difference.

Tactfulness and sincerity of purpose are inseparable twins—virtually Siamese twins for one is seldom found without the other.

Almost all of life is a matter of give and take. And you'll find that you can make a better bargain for yourself if you develop your powers of tactfulness as the most effective means of negotiating your way through life.

Anyone can become a tactful person. It's simply a matter of restraint and discretion, of putting reason and logic ahead of emotion, of trying to foresee the impact your words and deeds will have on others.

You'll find tactfulness comes easier to you if you learn to ask yourself these questions before speaking in important situations:

"Suppose I were the other person—how would I want to hear what I am about to say—what words would I want to hear to soften the meaning? How can I turn the meaning into something he will want to hear?"

In every situation the most variable factor will be the other person. You must be able to judge his or her character and personality quickly and accurately before deciding on a course of words or action. The same situation involving different persons might require entirely different solutions.

Tactfulness, for example, was the only tool the late Dr. William Harper, president of the University of Chicago, used to pry $1,000,000 for a new campus building from a man who was especially tough to approach for donations.

Knowing a blunt request would result in quick rejection, Dr. Harper studied his man carefully. He learned that in addition to having much money, the man had a lengthy list of business adversaries he delighted in out-foxing.

"I want to tell you," Harper told the man, "that I took the liberty of putting your name in nomination for the honor of donating the new building to the campus. The trustees will choose the donor tomorrow."

"What makes you think I want the honor?" the man asked.

OTHER NAMES HELP

"Perhaps you're right," Harper said, preparing to leave. "Thanks for your time. We have four other names in nomination anyway."

The four he named included one of the man's most bitter rivals. The business man was shocked.

"Could you arrange for me to speak to the trustees before they vote?" he asked. Dr. Harper said he could.

As a result, the man appeared the next day with a $1,000,000 check in hand, begging for the chance to contribute the money. The trustees weren't too hard to convince.

You can also use tactfulness to give others a burning desire to help you achieve your goal.

LEND LESS LUCKY A
HELPING HAND

Some people think it's impossible to make money—to achieve success—without depriving others of it. Nothing could be further from the truth.

The truly great fortunes are amassed by men with the vision and courage to create a better service or product, which, in turn, creates jobs, investment opportunities, sales and wealth for large groups of people.

Nevertheless, the American system of economics is based—and rightly so—on competition.

To be successful, you must learn to conduct yourself properly under competitive conditions between people, companies, products and services.

You must bring to this arena the same high standards of behavior that apply on the athletic field.

HELP OTHER FELLOW

Remember first of all that no man climbs to success on the shoulders of another. You stand or fall on your own merits and your own contributions.

Elbert Hubbard once wrote: "There is so much good in the worst of us and so much bad in the best of us that it does not behoove any of us to speak ill of the rest of us."

"If you slander someone, do not speak it," Hubbard said. "Write it—in the sands near the water's edge."

Good sportsmanship is a positive quality rather than passive.

Instead of merely refraining from kicking the other fellow when he's down, we should give him a helping hand to get back on his feet.

Your attitude should be the same in victory or defeat. For the quitter never wins and the winner never quits.

TRUE SPORTSMANSHIP

It's in moments of blackest adversity that the true sportsman shows the greatest courage and fighting spirit. And in the flush of victory he shows the most solicitude for those he left behind in the race.

The mark of the true leader is not so much his greater courage, strength or intelligence. It shows in his concern for those less favorably endowed by nature or circumstance.

You can demonstrate your ability—and right—to lead others by exercising the extra measure of sportsmanship necessary to make their work a little easier and their existence a bit more comfortable.

Remember that when you smooth the road to success for others, you take the bumps out of it for yourself too.

Art Linkletter—of television and radio fame—sets a fine example.

ASSISTANCE PAID OFF

Besides his busy entertainment career, Art has his hands in literally scores of small businesses he has helped others establish with his investments, time, effort, advice—and encouragement.

As a result, he has interests in—and is receiving profits from—such diverse products and services as photo development, TV camera manufacturing, lead mines, a bowling alley and a skating rink.

The people he helped establish in these businesses know that Art is a real leader.

You can become the same kind of a leader through dynamic sportsmanship.

Don't just extend the hand of friendship to others. Make it a helping hand.

TRUE GRATITUDE
PAYS DIVIDENDS

Many successful men and women claim they are "self-made." But the fact is that no one reaches the pinnacle without help.

Once you have set your definite major goal for success—and taken your first steps to achieve it—you find yourself receiving help from many unexpected quarters.

You must be prepared to give thanks for both the human and the Divine help you receive.

Gratitude is a beautiful word. It is beautiful because it describes a state of mind that is deeply spiritual in nature. It enhances one's personality with magnetic charm, and it is the master key that opens the door to the magic powers and the beauty of Infinite Intelligence.

Gratitude, like other traits of the pleasing personality, is simply a matter of habit. But it's also a state of mind. Unless you sincerely feel the gratitude you express, your words will be hollow and empty—and sound as phony as the sentiment you offer.

GIVE THANKS DAILY

Gratitude and graciousness are closely akin. By consciously developing a sense of gratitude, your personality will become more courtly, dignified and gracious.

Never let a day pass without a few minutes spent in giving thanks for your blessings. Remember that gratitude is a matter of comparison. Compare circumstances and events against what they might have been. You'll become aware that no matter how bad things are, they could be much worse—and you'll be grateful they aren't.

Three phrases should be among the most common in your daily usage. They are: "Thank you," "I'm grateful," and "I appreciate . . ."

Be thoughtful. Try to find new and unique ways to express your gratitude. Not necessarily in material gifts, however, time and effort are more precious, and the amount of these you dispense in showing gratefulness will be well worthwhile.

THANK THOSE NEAR YOU

And don't forget to be thankful to those who are closest to you—your wife or husband, other relatives, and those you associate with daily, whom you might tend to neglect.

You are probably more indebted to them than you realize. Gratitude takes on new meaning—new life and power—when spoken aloud. Your family probably knows you are grateful for their faith and hope in you. But tell them so! Frequently you'll find a new spirit pervading the household.

Make your gratitude creative. Make it work for you.

For example, have you ever thought of writing the boss a simple note telling him how much you like your job and how grateful you are for the opportunities it offers? The shock power of such creative gratitude will bring you to his attention—and could even bring you a raise. Gratitude is infectious. He might catch the bug and find concrete ways of expressing his gratefulness for the good services you are rendering.

Remember there's always something to be grateful for. Even the prospect who turns down a salesman should be thanked for the time he spent listening. He'll be more likely to buy next time.

Gratitude costs nothing. But it's a big investment in the future.

HELPING OTHERS
ALSO HELPS YOU

All of us have met successful people who claim they are "self-made." Actually, there's no such thing as a completely self-made man or woman. People who make such claims only prove that it's possible for ingrates to make money.

Every person who reaches the top receives substantial boosts along the way from others. The simple law of the fair play required that he respond by helping others.

The turning point in my own career, for example, came when Andrew Carnegie advised me to begin organizing the Science of Success as a definitive philosophy of knowledge—and gave me his active help and support to do so. I hope that in passing on what I learned in a lifetime of research I am paying off the debt incurred when Carnegie lent me his aid so many decades ago.

You can further your own career by helping others achieve their goals. There is no greater truth than the wonderful epigram: "Help thy brother's boat across and lo! thine own hath reached the shore."

No man is more wealthy than the one who has the time and energy to spend in helping others. Notice, I didn't mention money. That's fine too for helping others if you can afford it. But time and effort is even more precious. And the pay-off in satisfaction and self-contentment is commensurate with the investment.

A RICH EXPERIENCE

One of the richest experiences you'll ever enjoy is to be able to point to someone at the peak of success and say: "I helped put him there."

Your efforts on behalf of someone less fortune not only help him, but add something of priceless value to your own soul—whether or not he recognizes your aid and whether or not he is grateful for it.

It's a strange fact that human nature seeks struggle, on behalf of either ourselves or others.

I remember how, when I was considerably younger, I finally fought free of debt. All my obligations were discharged. I was contented—or so I thought.

But as months passed, unrest set in. It took me some time to realize what was wrong. It was the fun of the fight I missed.

But that didn't mean I had to give up my own fortune and start from scratch again. I found I could get just as much fun out of helping others fight their battles by assuming some of their responsibilities, thereby making the way to success easier for them.

COULD TRANSFORM WORLD

Think how the world would be transformed if each of us "adopted" someone else to help through life! In turn, each of us would be adopted and receive help.

In a small way, it's already happening. But the system, if I may call it that, needs to be improved and expanded as part of human progress and civilization.

At the beginning of time, Man learned the answer to his question: "Am I my brother's keeper?"

The answer is more valid than ever today.

PUT MAGNETISM
INTO PERSONALITY

You have, no doubt, met persons to whom you are drawn irresistibly on initial contact—people you accept immediately as friends and trust far more than the average casual acquaintance.

All of us possess such personal magnetism—some more than others, but everyone to some degree.

Personal magnetism seems to be a biological inheritance that determines the amount of emotional feeling—such as enthusiasm, love and joy—we are capable of generating and applying in our words and deeds.

We can't increase the quality or quantity of this inheritance. But we can organize it and direct it to help us attain any desired aim. And those who learn to do so often become the leaders, the builders, the doers and the pioneers who help advance our civilization.

CAUTION CALLED FOR

Often—but not always. For it frequently happens that unworthy persons possess this great power to influence others. Therefore, it behooves us to apply an extra measure of caution when dealing with such persons until certain of their intentions and motives.

The important thing, however, is that you can put your personal magnetism to work for you to achieve success.

With it, you can obtain the friendly cooperation of others to help you attain your principal major goals.

Personal magnetism is revealed mainly through the voice, eyes and hands—in short, the principal means we have of communicating our thoughts and ideas to others. But your very bearing and posture play a part in it too.

ENTHUSIASM POTENT

The actual words used may be quite meaningless, but the tone of voice, force of delivery and enthusiasm with which they are given may be far more powerful than the logic and rhetoric they offer.

For that matter, a person possessing an extremely high degree of personal magnetism may not have to speak a word to draw people to his side.

An outstanding example is offered by the evangelist, the Rev. Billy Graham.

He draws souls relentlessly to the Creator by a mere

gesture with a glance from his expressive eyes, or through a melodiously voiced phrase.

Franklin Delano Roosevelt had the same power over others.

MISCREANTS ALSO HAVE IT

But, I must point out, so did Hitler, Mussolini and other unsavory leaders of history.

If you try consciously to use it, you can put this same power to work for you. Learn to use your eyes, hands and voice to exude self-confidence, spiritual strength and authority.

Make a conscious effort to meet the gaze of others more directly, to clasp their hands firmly and warmly, to speak in pleasant, forthright tones with volume pitched and timbre gauged to capture the interest of your listeners.

Turn on your personal magnetism and see what it can do for you!

SPIRITUAL OUTLOOK
KEY TO PROGRESS

Only the Devil refuses forgiveness. The Creator provides the means of forgiveness for everyone, living or dead. Can you afford to do less?

God's word repeatedly urges us to forgive . . . to turn the other cheek . . . to love one another . . . that vengeance is the Lord's and He will repay.

Your chances of material success in life depend greatly on your spiritual outlook.

The more positive your thinking, the greater your chances of success. Time and thought expended on yearning for vengeance are wasted.

There is a rule of business not to send good money after the bad. Effort and energy expended in trying to "get even" go down the drain the same way. How much better it is to exert ourselves constructively to new projects and goals rather than to burn out our spirits brooding over lost causes!

LAW OF COMPENSATION

Forgiveness isn't mere acquiescence to the behavior of others. It's more positive and active than that. In forgiving, we assume some of the contrition our offenders should feel.

Each time you forgive someone, you broaden the space your own soul occupies because that space is filled with the deed of generosity you perform. The universal law of compensation applies here more than ever, for even in our prayers we dare ask Divine forgiveness only in proportion to the forgiveness we bestow on our fellow men.

Forgiveness is a spiritual medicine that works two ways, healing the psychic wound of the offended person who grants it as well as relieving the penitence of the offender.

Forgiveness is the major tenet of Christianity, ordained to us in the Sermon on the Mount—"Blessed are the merciful . . ." and "Judge not, that ye be not judged; for with what judgment ye judge, ye shall be judged."

GOLDEN RULE BEST

These injunctions are fully as applicable to our material, as well as our spiritual lives. The best rule of business is The Golden Rule.

Most grievances are based purely on misunderstandings. Few people are consciously hurtful toward others. Too often we stand on our "rights" instead of on our "duties." Every setback at the hands of others can be turned to account.

I can vouch for this story—for I was the lecturer. Let me give an example.

A lecturer was boycotted by a public leader in a small Missouri town because he didn't like the lecturer's sponsor. When the lecturer heard about it, he "retaliated" by using his lecture fee of several thousand dollars to buy radio time so everyone in town could hear the series free. His unique way of "striking back" so impressed his opponent that he gladly gave his endorsement to the lecturer.

The result was a completely new spirit of constructiveness throughout the town. Old animosities were wiped out. The idea of cooperation and helpfulness caught fire. The entire character of the town changed. New projects were touched off. Business boomed and the community enjoyed a prosperity it had never known before.

ALL ARE HELPED BY
COMPETITION

Healthy competition is the mainspring of business in our country. It inspires everyone to put their utmost into their daily work. Human nature is such that without competition men and women tend to hit a dead level of mediocrity.

Perhaps can illustrate my point best with a parable that happens to be true.

Norton, Virginia, was a sleepy little village at the turn of the century. The storekeepers—they could hardly be called merchants—spent most of their time around pot-bellied stoves swapping yarns with village loafers. Their show windows offered more dirt and cobwebs than merchandise, and customers often had to wait on themselves because proprietors were too busy with their checker games.

Then one day a little peddler by the name of Ike Kauffman showed up with a pack of merchandise on his back almost outweighing himself.

For months Ike peddled his wares up and down the

Guest and Powell rivers, getting acquainted with everyone in the mountain country.

IKE WAKES 'EM UP

Local merchants didn't take him seriously. They called him "the little pack rat"—until the day when carpenters began work on a store building two stories high and three times bigger than the largest store in town.

Merchandise began arriving by the carload—and there was Ike Kauffman, arranging the finest assortment of general wares the people of Wise County had ever seen.

When the store opened for business, great crowds of customers came daylong to visit it. Norton had never seen the like. For while Ike was selling wares up country, he also was making friends. And a week before the store opened, he sent invitations to all of them to be his guest at "Norton's Biggest and Newest Merchandise Emporium."

Local merchants were goggle-eyed at the sight of his attractive, clean and artful displays.

SO THEY GET BUSY

They got busy, cleaned up their own shops and began dressing up their show windows. Some built new stores and stocked them with new lines of merchandise.

As a result, Norton enjoyed a major business boom with competition as the powerful motivating force.

But the story doesn't end there. One cold winter night,

the entire business section, including Ike's new store, burned to the ground. A short time earlier, that might have meant "the death of the village."

But the spirit of competition was so great that business men raced to rebuild modern structures. The village grew so fast that it soon became a "town" and then the thriving, prosperous city it is today.

Ike Kauffman died and was buried and forgotten by all but a few old-timers who saw him transform a drowsy country hamlet into a modern city. But he shouldn't be forgotten!

Norton should erect a monument to "Ike Kauffman, the man who taught us the value of clean competition."

You can benefit also if you learn to accept competition as a blessing, rather than a curse.

Remember it is only by judging you against your competitors that people who pay for your services—your employer or customers—can measure the value of your performance and qualifications.

ANALYZING SELF HELPS
IN CLIMB

Frequent critical self-analysis is necessary to insure that you are adhering to the principles that can carry you to the heights of success.

Perhaps a check list will help you find the weak points that are impeding you. Try comparing yourself to an imaginary success-bound person—let's call him Joe Smith—and see how you stack up.

Joe has set a definite goal in life for himself and laid out a plan for attaining it within a definite time limit. In short, he's taken the first and most important step toward success. Have you?

And each time Joe meets a temporary defeat, instead of becoming discouraged, he searches for the seed of equivalent benefit one can always find to turn events in his favor.

Joe lives each day with zest and enthusiasm that makes play of his work. He refrains from talking "poor mouth"—from discussing his troubles with others—knowing that success is bred by the very sound of success.

HE "GOES THE EXTRA MILE"

He constantly "goes the extra mile," rendering more and better service than expected.

Moreover, he knows that greater success can be obtained by the group than by the individual. He eagerly seeks cooperative alliance in which a free exchange of ideas, talents and energies will more certainly result in the desired goals.

Joe dresses appropriately. He budgets his income and carefully sets aside some of it in savings. He guards his health, by living moderately.

Above all, Joe maintains a perpetually positive mental attitude. The word "impossible" isn't in his vocabulary.

BELIEVES FIRST PRINCIPLE

Joe is convinced of the truth of the first principle of the Science of Success: "Whatever the mind of Man can conceive and believe, the mind can achieve."

He makes sure that all parties to a transaction benefit by it—there isn't any winner or loser.

He's loyal. He avoids disparaging others because such remarks are as negative to him as to those he talks about. Instead, he goes out of his way to give compliments and praise—not flattery—where they are due.

His superior and his subordinates too admire Joe Smith because he makes prompt decisions and takes full responsibility for them. He never passes the buck in either direction.

ALL MEN HIS BROTHERS

Joe's a likable guy to be with. He has a sense of humor, thoughtfulness for others, and practices courtesy to everyone. He never uses objectionable language. He regards all men as his brothers.

He tries constantly to improve himself. He knows that good books, good plays, good art can be enjoyed with little expense in libraries, museums and repertory theaters. Most important, he makes steady use of these facilities.

Joe is dependable and prompt. His word is his bond. His credit is good because he knows that too much debt is a millstone that would drag him back as he climbs the ladder of success.

How do you compare to Joe?

SHAKING HANDS CAN BE A HELP

Your voice, your eyes and your hands tell people what sort of a person you are. Your handshake can convince new acquaintances that you are someone worth knowing better. Every successful salesman knows the value of a good "proper" handclasp. With it, he communicates warmth, friendliness, enthusiasm and confidence.

You should learn to use your handshake to help sell your way through life.

Our ritual of grasping each other's hand on being introduced has a very sound psychological, social and spiritual basis. Through it, we signify our kindredness with other men, our willingness to accept them as equals, our respect and affection for all men.

CLIMAX OF RITUAL

Like any form of communication, it must be practiced and used frequently to be effective. Some persons have a "natural" handshake. But anyone can develop one by deliberate cultivation.

Actually, the clasp of hands is the climax—the culminating act—of the meeting ritual.

Learn, on being introduced to someone, to put a friendly smile in your eyes as well as on your lips—and words will be unnecessary to tell how glad you are to meet him.

Meet his handclasp firmly—but not vigorously or energetically. And by all means avoid the pumping type of handshake that turns this act of friendship into a caricature.

LESSON IN T.R.

President Theodore Roosevelt learned a lesson at his first New Year's Day reception in the White House. His hand was so badly crushed by enthusiastic hand pumpers he couldn't use it for a week! The next New Year's he used a trick to ease wear and tear. Each time he extended his hand, he folded two fingers to the palm so the greeter had only his first and second finger to damage!

Once a young lawyer seeking a pardon for a client was introduced to Woodrow Wilson by the late Sen. J. Hamilton Lewis of Illinois. The attorney, eager to please, squeezed Wilson's hand so tightly Wilson lost his aplomb, snatched his hand away and said, "You know better than that!" The young man didn't get the pardon he sought.

HANDSHAKE TRADEMARK

You can make your handshake your trademark—as Franklin D. Roosevelt did with his trick of taking the other person's hand in both of his, or Harry Truman with his mannerism of crossed arms for double handshake with two persons at a time.

Mrs. Eleanor Roosevelt once wrote: "Let me shake hands with a person and watch the expression on his face— and I can tell you a great deal about his character."

Your handclasp may seem like a small unimportant detail. But with it you may someday grasp a hand that can pull you to the pinnacle of success.

OVERCOME FEAR TO
REACH GOAL

Fear is the greatest single obstacle to success. Too often, people let fear rule all their decisions and actions. Their every yearning is for a sort of overall protection summed up in the catch-all cliché of "security."

The truly successful person doesn't think in these terms. His reasoning is based on creativeness and productivity. As President Eisenhower said, "One can attain a high degree of security in a prison cell if that's all he wants out of life."

The successful person is one who is willing to take risks when sound logic shows they are necessary to reach the desired goal.

SUFFER FROM FEAR

All of us suffer from fear. What is it? Fear is an emotion intended to help preserve our lives by warning us of danger.

Hence, fear can be a blessing when it raises its flag of

caution so we pause and study a situation before making a decision or taking action.

We must control fear rather than permit it to control us. Once it has served its emotional purpose as a warning signal, we must not permit it to enter into the logical reasoning by which we decide upon a course of action.

FDR's famous words—"We have nothing to fear but fear itself"—are as applicable now and at any time as when he uttered them during the Depression.

ROAD OF REASON

How can you overcome your fears? First of all, by looking them full in the face—by consciously saying: "I am afraid." And then ask yourself: "Of what?"

With that one question you have begun analyzing the situation facing you. You are on the road of reason that will carry you around the emotional obstacle of fear.

The next step is to consider the problem from every facet. What are the risks? Is the expected reward worth taking them? What are the other possible courses of action? What unexpected problems are likely to be encountered? Do you have all the necessary data, statistics and facts at hand? What have others done in similar situations, and what were the results?

Once you have completed your study, take action—immediately! Procrastination leads only to more doubt and fear.

FIRST STEP IMPORTANT

A noted psychologist once said that a woman, alone at night and imagining she hears noises, can settle her fears quickly. All she has to do is put one foot on the floor. In doing so, she has taken the first step on a positive course of action toward overcoming her fear.

The person seeking success must force himself in the same way to control his fear by taking the first step toward his goal.

And remember that no one walks the road of life alone.

One of the most consoling—and truest—assurances given us is found in the Bible: "Fear not, I am with you always."

Faith in those words will give you spiritual strength to meet any situation.

FEARS MASTERED
BY OPEN MINDS

One of the best ways to overcome fear—the greatest obstacle to success—is to ask yourself bluntly: "What am I afraid of?"

Often it turns out that we are shying at mere shadows.

Let's examine some of the most common worries and see how this system works.

Sickness—The human body is endowed with an ingenious system for automatic self-maintenance and repair. Why worry then that it might get out of order? It is better to marvel at how it stays in proper working order, in spite of the demands we place upon it!

Old Age—The Golden Years are something to look forward to—not to fear. We exchange youth for wisdom. Remember, nothing is ever taken away from us without an equal or greater benefit being made available.

FAILURE MAY BE BLESSING

Failure—Momentary failure is a blessing in disguise, carrying with it the seed of an equivalent benefit if we but seek to learn its cause and use our knowledge to better our effort on the next attempt.

Death—Recognize that it is a necessary part of the overall plan of the universe, provided by the Creator as a means of giving man a passageway to the higher plane of Eternity.

Criticism—You should, after all, be your own most severe critic. What, then, can you fear in the criticism of others? And such criticism may include constructive suggestions that will help you better yourself.

Fear results mainly from ignorance.

LIGHTNING ONCE FEARED

Man feared the lightning until Franklin, Edison and a few other rare individuals, who dared to take possession of their own minds, proved that lightning is a form of physical energy that could be harnessed for the benefit of humanity.

We can master fear easily if we will but open our minds through Faith to the guidance of Divine Intelligence.

Looking about us in nature, we discover a universal plan through which every living creature has been wisely and benevolently provided with food and all other necessities of their existence.

Is it likely, then, that man—chosen as the master of every other species on earth—would be neglected?

PAIN A PART OF PLAN

Even physical pain, which many persons fear unreasonably, plays a part in the plan, for it is a universal language by which the most uneducated person knows when he is endangered by injury or illness.

What right have we in the light of this to go to the Creator with prayers over petty matters which we could and should settle for ourselves? How dare we, if these prayers go unanswered, lose what little faith we may have possessed?

Perhaps the greatest sin lies in loss of faith in the all-wise Creator who has provided His children with more blessings than any earthly parent could ever hope to give his offspring.

YOUR MIND HAS
HIDDEN POWERS

Locked within the human mind lie powers beyond comprehension. The imagination is the key which can release them to work for the individual and for humanity.

Only a few of the millions upon millions of men through the ages have recognized this fact and used it to direct their own destinies.

The imagination is our gateway of approach to the infinite intelligence of the Creator. It is opened by the state of mind known as Faith.

It is in this state of mind that hope and purpose are translated into physical reality. For it is a fact that all thought tends to transform itself into its physical equivalent.

Faith provides the imagination with the stimulative capacity of desire and enthusiasm with which one's plans and purposes may be given action.

FAITH IN SELF

Through faith in himself, any person can achieve any goal he desires.

Henry Ford once was asked what type of men he needed most for his company.

"I could use a hundred men who don't know there is such a word as 'impossible,'" he replied.

And it has been said that Ford's stupendous business success resulted from two personal traits: (1) He set himself a definite major goal in life and then (2) recognized no limitation in pursuit of his aim.

The imagination is the workshop of the soul wherein every man can shape his own earthly destiny.

Truly, whatever the mind can conceive and believe, the mind can achieve.

Clarence Saunders, working as a grocery clerk, conceived the idea for a self-service type of grocery merchandising plan.

He was convinced the idea would pay off and offered to share it with his boss. The boss, lacking Saunders' imagination, promptly fired him for "wasting time with foolish ideas."

Four years later, Saunders launched his famed Piggly Wiggly stores which yielded him more than $4,000,000.

Andrew Carnegie, who first encouraged me to develop the "Science of Success," used to say, "You can do it if you believe you can."

But it takes will power, too. Sometimes amounting to sheer bullheadedness.

YOUR IMAGINATION

Clarence Saunders might have been tempted to give up the idea for a "cafeteria-style" grocery store if his will power had not impelled him to keep going—even though it had cost him his job.

Your imagination will help you achieve success if you give it a chance.

But once it has done its work, you alone can apply the faith and will power to make your dreams come true.

Don't make the mistake of eating the husk of fear and throwing away the rich kernels of abundance and plenty.

Ask yourself now: "What am I afraid of?" The answer probably will be "Nothing."

FIND HAPPINESS
IN AIDING OTHERS

The richest man in all the world lives over in Happy Valley. He is rich in values that endure, in things he cannot lose—things that provide him with contentment, sound health, peace of mind and harmony within his soul.

Here is an inventory of his riches and how he acquired them: "I found happiness by helping others to find it.

"I found sound health by living temperately and eating only the food my body requires to maintain itself.

"I am free from all causes and effects of fear and worry.

"I hate no man, envy no man, but love and respect all mankind. I am engaged in a labor of love with which I mix play generously; therefore, I never grow tired.

"I pray daily, not for more riches, but for more wisdom with which to recognize, embrace and enjoy the great abundance of riches I already possess.

"I speak no name save only to honor it, and I slander no man for any cause whatsoever."

SHARE BLESSINGS

"I ask no favors of anyone except the privilege of sharing my blessings with all who desire them.

"I am on good terms with my conscience, therefore, it guides me accurately in everything I do.

"I have no enemies because I injure no man. Rather, I try to help everyone with whom I come in contact.

"I have more material wealth than I need because I am free from greed and covet only those things I can use constructively while I live. My wealth comes from those whom I have benefited by sharing my blessings.

"The estate of Happy Valley which I own is not taxable. It exists mainly in my own mind, in intangible riches that cannot be assessed for taxation or appropriated except by those who adopt my way of life. I created this estate over a lifetime of effort by observing nature's law and forming habits to conform with them." There are no copyrights on the Happy Valley Man's success creed.

If you will adopt it, and live by it, you can make life pay off on your own terms.

It can attract to you new and more desirable friends, as well as disarm enemies.

It can help you to occupy more space in the world and get more joy from living.

IT CAN MEAN PROSPERITY

It can bring prosperity to your business profession or calling, and make your home a paradise of profound enjoyment for every member of your family.

It can add years to your life and give you freedom from fear and anxiety.

It can place you on the "success beam" and keep you there.

But above all, the Happy Valley Man's creed can bring you wisdom to solve all your personal problems—before they arise—and give you peace and contentment.

STUDIED SILENCE
OFTEN BEATS TALK

Everyone agrees that the ability to speak frankly can help make a person a success. Men such as Billy Graham, Franklin Roosevelt and Winston Churchill propelled themselves to the top through their ability to sway large masses with their oratory.

But there is a time also when studied silence is equally important. The secret here is in being a good listener.

Nowhere is this more true than in salesmanship.

One of this country's top life insurance salesmen never undertakes to make a presentation until he has made his prospective buyer talk by asking him these questions:

1. If you should pass away today, have you accumulated enough money to take care of your family the way you want them cared for?
2. Are your assets of a type that your family could not lose to dishonest persons?
3. How much insurance do you carry?
4. How many children have you and what are their ages?

Through diplomatic handling of the answers to these four questions, this expert salesman knows when to take over and begin talking. More important, he knows precisely what to say in order to make a sale.

All master salesmen use this question method to arm themselves with effective material for rebuttals when their prospects put up arguments. As a result, the prospective buyer often talks himself into an indefensible position where his resistance is bound to fail. Sometimes, he talks himself into making the purchase.

One very successful saleswoman has built a lucrative organization through "qualifying" people, by telephone, as prospective buyers of real estate, stocks and bonds, insurance and a great variety of other commodities and services.

She starts off by asking questions that can be answered, usually only in the way she wants them answered. For example, if selling stocks and bonds, she starts off:

"Mr. Businessman, would you be interested in learning how you could earn money without working for it?"

Since any person would, the answer usually is "yes." Her next question is:

"What sum of money do you wish to earn without working for it?"

Upon getting an answer, the prospect is told that a salesman will see him in person and tell him how the money can be earned.

This clever woman has even recruited salesmen themselves to sell certain products by calling their wives and asking:

"Mrs. Housewife, would you be interested in learning how your husband can increase his income so you can have a better home, a new car, a mink coat and money to travel wherever you want to go?"

The wife becomes so enthusiastic it's easy to make a date, through her, for management to interview her husband.

Socrates, one of history's greatest thinkers, used the question method to put his ideas across. So did Plato and other philosophers.

Induce the other fellow to talk freely and you will know what to say—and how to say it—when your turn comes to speak.

HOW TO GET OFF
"FAILURE BEAM"

It's often said that the rich tend constantly to become richer and the poor to become poorer. My own studies of the principles which make some persons immediately successful and others abject failures seem to bear this out.

The Bible puts it this way: "He that hath shall be given, and he shall have abundance; but from him that hath not shall be taken away even that which he hath." (Matthew)

It is also a fact that possessions are to be used, not hoarded. Whatever we own—we must use it or lose it.

ETERNAL CHANGE

Strange also is the fact that only one thing is permanent in this universe—eternal change. Nothing remains exactly the same for even a second. Even the physical body in which we live changes completely with astonishing rapidity.

You can test these statements against your own experience. When a person is struggling for recognition and to get a few dollars ahead, seldom will he find anyone to give him a needed lift. But once he makes the grade—and no longer needs help—people stand in line to offer him aid.

Through what I call the law of attraction, like attracts like in all circumstances. Success attracts greater success. Failure attracts more failure.

Throughout our lives we are the beneficiaries or victims of a swiftly flowing stream which carries us onward toward either success or failure.

The idea is to get on the "success beam" rather than on the "failure beam."

How can you do this? Simple. The answer lies in adopting a positive mental attitude that will help you shape the course of your own destiny rather than drifting along at the mercy of life's adversities.

POWER TO THINK

Your mind has been endowed with the power to think, to aspire, to hope, to direct your life toward any goal you seek. It is the one and only thing over which we have the complete, unchallenged privilege of control.

But remember, we must embrace this prerogative—and use it—or suffer severe penalties. Truly, whatever it is we possess—material, mental or spiritual—we must use it or lose it.

First, clearly define to yourself the position you wish to attain in life. Then say to yourself: "I can do it . . . I can do it now."

Chart the steps you must take to reach your goal. Take

them one at a time and you will find that with each piece-meal success the next step comes easier and easier as more people are attracted to help you achieve your ultimate purpose.

Remember that you cannot stand still. You must move upwards toward success—or downwards toward failure.

The choice is yours alone.

SERVING OTHERS
WILL HELP YOU

One of the surest ways to achieve your own success in life is by helping others to attain theirs. Almost anyone can contribute money toward those less fortunate.

But the truly affluent person is the one who can afford to give of himself, of his time and energy, to the benefit of others. In so doing he enriches himself beyond measure.

John Wanamaker, the Philadelphia merchant king, once said that the most profitable habit was that of "rendering useful service where it is not expected."

And Edward Bok, the great editor of the *Ladies' Home Journal*, said he rose from poverty to wealth through the practice of "making myself useful to others, without regard to what I received in return."

HELPING TAKES EFFORT

It takes conscious effort to give your time and energy to others. You can't simply say, "All right, I'm willing to help anyone who needs my help." You must make a creative project of rendering a service to your fellow men.

Perhaps some down-to-earth examples will help you think of ways you can win friends by helping others.

There is, for instance, a merchant in an eastern city who has built up a very successful business through a very simple process.

Every hour or so one of his clerks checks the parking meters near the store.

PENNIES WIN FRIENDS

Where the clerk spots an "expired" sign he drops a penny in the slot, and attaches a note to the car telling the owner that the merchant has been happy to protect him against the inconvenience of a traffic ticket. Many motorists drop in to thank the merchant—and remain to buy.

The owner of a big Boston men's store inserts a neatly printed card in the pocket of each suit he sells. It tells the purchaser that if he finds the suit satisfactory, he may bring the card back after six months and exchange it for any necktie he chooses.

Naturally, the buyer always comes back pleased with the suit—and is a ripe prospect for another sale.

The highest paid woman employee of the Bankers Trust Co. in New York City got her start by offering to work three months without pay in order to demonstrate her executive ability.

And Butler Stork gave of himself so freely as a prisoner

in the Ohio State Penitentiary that he was released, beating a 20-year sentence for forgery.

Stork organized a correspondence school that taught more than 1,000 inmates a variety of courses without charge to them or the state. He even induced the International Correspondence School to donate textbooks.

The plan attracted so much attention that Stork was given his freedom as a reward.

Put your own mind to work. Assess your own ability and energy. Who needs your help? How can you help them? It doesn't take money. All it takes is ingenuity and a strong desire to be of genuine service.

Helping others solve their problems will help you solve your own.

AVOID PITFALLS
CAUSING FAILURE

Anyone who aspires to success in life must recognize the causes of failure. Else how can he avoid pitfalls? In my researches into human relations, I have found at least 30 major causes of failure.

But the grand-daddy of them all is the lack of ability to get along harmoniously with others.

A great business man—one of the wealthiest men of his day—once told me that he had a five-point measuring stick he used in choosing men for the advancement to high executive jobs.

1. A faculty for getting along with others.
2. Loyalty to those to whom loyalty is due.
3. Dependability under all circumstances.
4. Patience in all situations.
5. Ability to do a given job well.

ABILITY PLACED LAST

It is notable that "ability for the job" came last. That's because the more ability a man has for a task, the more objectionable he may be if he lacks the other four traits.

Charles M. Schwab was promoted by Andrew Carnegie from day laborer to a $75,000-a-year job. In addition, Carnegie gave Schwab a bonus that sometimes reached $1,000,000 a year.

Carnegie said the salary was for the actual service Schwab rendered. But the bonus was for what he inspired other workers to do.

Your ability to inspire others is a blank check on the Bank of Life that you can fill in for whatever you desire.

If you lack this ability, you can take steps now to acquire it.

GO OUT OF YOUR WAY

How? By adopting and following these rules:

1. Go out of your way, at least once daily, to speak a kind word or render some useful service where it is not expected.
2. Modify your voice to convey a feeling of warmth and friendship to those you address.
3. Direct your conversation to subjects of the greatest interest to your listeners. Talk "with" them rather than "to" them. Consider the person with whom you're conversing as the most interesting in the world, at least at that moment.

4. Soften your expression frequently with a smile as you speak.

5. Never, under any circumstances, use profanity or obscenity.

6. Keep your religious and political views to yourself.

BE WARY OF ASKING

7. Never ask a favor of anyone you haven't yourself helped at some time previous.

8. Be a good listener. Inspire others to speak freely on subjects that interest them.

9. Never speak disparagingly of other people. Don't "talk poor mouth." Remember that an ounce of optimism is worth a ton of pessimism.

10. Close each day with this prayer: "I ask not for more blessings, but more wisdom with which to make better use of the blessings I now possess. And give me, please, more understanding that I may occupy more space in the hearts of my fellow men by rendering more service tomorrow than I have rendered today."

BELIEF BRINGS MIGHTY POWER

You have at your command the mightiest power in the universe—your capacity for belief. In truth, this is the only power you are completely and irrevocably privileged to control and direct for purposes of your own choice.

The world's most immensely successful people are those who recognize and use their capacity for belief.

They believe in the power of Infinite Intelligence. They believe in their right to draw upon this power and direct it to ends of their own choice. They know that with it, all things are possible. The word "impossible" doesn't exist for them.

But the power of belief is not flicked on and off like electric current. It must be nurtured and strengthened through everyday use.

The succeeding column will describe in detail a Daily Creed you can adopt as your own to help you develop your power of belief.

TALKS SELF TO SUCCESS

But for the moment, let's examine how one man achieved tremendous success through this power.

Edwin C. Barnes set a seemingly impossible goal as his major purpose in life. He decided he would become the business partner of the great Thomas A. Edison! And starting from scratch—with nothing to aid him but his capacity for belief—he literally "talked himself" into a plan to achieve his aim.

Every day, while gazing at his own face in a mirror, he made a speech to himself. The speech was spoken aloud. It was definite.

And Barnes delivered it with all the enthusiasm he could muster.

"Mr. Edison," Barnes would say, "you are going to accept me as your business partner and I am going to be so useful to you that the rewards will make me rich."

SATURATES HIS BRAIN

In this way, Barnes literally saturated his brain with unshakable belief that he would become Edison's partner.

Consequently, when he presented his case to the great inventor, his enthusiasm was so boundless that Edison caught its spirit and gave him a trial—not as a partner, but as a salesman of the Edison dictating machine.

Barnes could have let disappointment crush him. But

he didn't. Instead, he grasped the opportunity presented to him.

He simply diverted his enthusiastic belief in himself to the task at hand. As a result, he was such a successful salesman that Edison was forced to take him into a partnership to distribute the machines nationally.

SECRET WAS SIMPLE

It wasn't long before everyone knew the slogan: "Made by Edison, sold by Barnes."

The partnership made Barnes a multi-millionaire. The secret of his success was simple: "Definiteness of purpose expressed with enthusiasm and enduring belief."

The next column will tell how you can develop these qualities to achieve your goal in life.

BELIEF IN SELF IS VERY VITAL

Success is achieved by those who are thoroughly imbued with belief that they can attain it. They are convinced of one fact: "Whatever my mind can conceive and believe, my mind can achieve!"

They consciously work to develop belief in themselves and their capability to realize any goal they set for themselves.

You can do the same, just as Edwin C. Barnes did when he conditioned his mind to a single aim—to become the business partner of the great inventor, Thomas A. Edison.

Barnes developed his tremendous power of belief by daily repetition of a creed, subsequently published in a bestselling book.

The same creed has been credited with helping men and women throughout the world to attain prosperity and peace of mind they previously would have considered impossible.

GREATEST WISHES

Repeating this creed to yourself at least once a day will help you to realize your greatest wishes, too. Here it is:

1. I will channel my mind toward prosperity and success by keeping my thoughts as much as possible upon the major goal I have set for myself.

2. I will free my mind of self-made limitations by drawing upon the power of Infinite Intelligence through unlimited faith.

3. I will keep my mind free of greed and covetousness by sharing my blessings with those who are worthy to receive them.

4. I will substitute a positive type of discontentment for indolent self-satisfaction so I may continue to learn and grow both physically and spiritually.

5. I will keep an open mind, on all subjects and toward all people, so I may rise above intolerance.

AVOID SELF-PITY

6. I will look for good in others and school myself to deal gently with their faults.

7. I will avoid self-pity. Under all circumstances I will seek stimulation to greater effort.

8. I will recognize and respect the difference between the material things I need and desire, and my *rights* to receive them.

9. I will cultivate the habit of "going the extra mile"—always rendering more and better service than is expected of me.

10. I will turn adversity and defeat into assets by remembering

that they always carry with them the seed of equivalent benefits.

11. I will always conduct myself toward others in such manner that I may never be ashamed to face the man I greet at the mirror each morning.

12. Finally, my daily prayer will be for wisdom to recognize and live my life in harmony with the overall purpose of the Creator.

Repeating this creed every day will soak it into your subconscious mind and make it part of your character. Through it you will develop attributes that will help you to attain a pleasing personality—our next subject of discussion.

MUCH DEPENDS ON
PERSONALITY

Every material or spiritual blessing you need or want is yours—if you learn to live harmoniously with your fellow man!

A pleasing personality is the greatest single asset you can possess. It is a key that will unlock doors to the friendship of others. It can disarm enemies and bring them to your side.

Many people believe that you must be born with a pleasing personality. You either have it, or you don't have it, they say. But that's not so. A pleasing personality can be developed through conscious endeavor to attain those traits of character, good manners, and concern for others that make us attractive spiritually to others.

We will examine these traits more extensively in future columns. But first, it might be well for you to assess your present personality—to see whether you are yourself a person with whom you would like daily contact.

YARDSTICK SET UP

Perhaps the best way to do this is by setting up a yardstick based on those personality features that all of us agree are the most objectionable. I've listed 17 of them here. It might be well to have yourself checked on these points by the person who knows you best:

1. Do you make sure that a conversation is two-sided, that the other person gets ample chance to speak, that you don't monopolize the talk and turn it into a monologue?
2. In conversation, do you put heavy emphasis on yourself and your personal interests?
3. Do you reveal yourself, by word or deed, as a selfish person?
4. Do you indulge in sarcasm and disparaging insinuations about others?
5. Do you exaggerate, revealing an uncontrolled imagination?

ONLY DEEDS COUNT

6. Are you vain? Are you guilty of actual or implied self-praise, forgetting that deeds—not words—are the only true means of self-elevation?
7. Are you indifferent toward others and their personal interests? Remember, the most important person living, at the moment, is the one with whom you are speaking—always.
8. Do you try to minimize the virtues and capabilities of others?
9. Do you use ingratiating flattery?

10. Do you try to talk over the heads of others just to convey a snob impression of superiority?

11. Do you lapse into insincerity (possibly in the form of flattery) in a phony attempt to please?

CHEAP GOSSIP

12. Do you indulge in cheap gossip or other forms of slander?

13. Are you slovenly in your dress, posture, or manner of speaking? Do you curse, use obscenity or profanity, or let poor slang weaken the forcefulness of your argument?

14. Do you try to attract attention unnecessarily, especially when it is someone else's turn to be the center of attraction?

15. Do you tread unnecessarily on the dangerous conversational grounds involved in such controversial subjects as race, religion, and politics when such subjects are obviously out of place?

16. Do you look for arguments just for the sake of arguments?

17. Do you bore and depress your listeners by constantly talking "poor mouth" by telling of your ailments, misfortunes, and strong personal dislikes?

By frankly admitting your failings in this list—and vowing to correct them—you will take a long step toward developing a pleasing personality. If you do this, you will be ready for the future columns which will teach you positive methods of attracting friends who can help you attain any goal you desire.

HOW TO DEVELOP
"FLEXIBLE WAY"

The normal individual wants to be liked. He wants the approbation and friendship of others. More than that, he knows that unless he can win the close, friendly cooperation of his associates, it will be difficult for him to achieve success in life.

The number one trait of a pleasing personality is flexibility.

It consists of the ability to "unbend" mentally and physically, to adapt one's self in any circumstance or environment while maintaining self-control and composure.

But the word does not denote pliability. You need not let yourself be subject to the whims and wiles of others in order to have a flexible mentality. Few people appreciate a "yes man."

ABILITY TO SURVEY

Flexibility can perhaps best be described as the ability to survey and assess a given situation swiftly and react to it on the basis of logic and reason with a minimum of emotion.

By developing flexibility you are prepared to take prompt action in seizing opportunities—or solving problems. It can help you become decisive.

Henry J. Kaiser's dramatic success in a wide variety of business enterprises is due very largely to his flexible mental attitude, which permits him to meet an unending flow of problems without ever being thrown off balance.

Flexibility also helped Arthur Nash, a Cincinnati mail order clothier, to adjust swiftly to the situation when his business went bankrupt. He took all his employees into partnership with him on a profit-sharing-plus-wages basis—and rebuilt the firm into one of the most profitable of its kind.

Sometimes, the flexibility of others can help you. For example, Henry Ford tended to be abrupt and short of patience with employees and business associates. Often, the flexible diplomacy of his wife, Clara, influenced him to forbearance and saved him many difficulties.

FOUR TRAITS

The head of the great Bank of America on the West Coast once said: "When we hire men and women we rate them by four traits—loyalty, dependability, flexibility and ability to do a given job well."

A sense of humor is an important ingredient in connection with flexibility. Abraham Lincoln often had to rely on his own native good spirits to hold his temperamental Cabinet members together in moments of crisis.

Humility—as distinguished from the Uriah type of

humbleness—also is necessary. Else how can you ever achieve that great degree of flexibility necessary to voice the words "I was wrong"—as everyone must someday?

Lack of such flexibility cost President Woodrow Wilson the Senate's approval of his cherished League of Nations project—and broke his heart. If he had throttled his pride and invited the late Senator Lodge—the League's chief opponent—to the White House for a conference, he might have won the Senate's sanction.

Flexibility is the one trait that softens poverty and adorns riches for it helps you to be grateful for your blessings and unabashed by misfortune. It can help you, too, to make beneficial use of every experience of life, whether pleasant or unpleasant.

BE ENTHUSIASTIC
AND ATTAIN GOAL

Ralph Waldo Emerson once said: "Nothing great is ever achieved without enthusiasm." And frequent repetition has not blemished the truth of the old statement that "nothing is so catching as enthusiasm."

Enthusiasm is the "radio wave" by which you transmit your personality to other persons. It is more powerful than logic, reason or rhetoric in getting your ideas across and in winning others to your viewpoint.

A highly successful sales manager says enthusiasm is the single most important trait of a good salesman—provided it is sincere and forthright.

"When you shake hands, put something extra into it that will make the other fellow feel you are genuinely happy to see him," he says.

SHUN PHONY ENTHUSIASM

A word of caution is necessary. Nothing is quite so phony as false enthusiasm—the excessively energetic, overwhelming display that bears its own stamp of falsity.

An example of how your own enthusiasm can carry you to the heights of great success is afforded in the career of Jennings Randolph.

After graduating at Salem College in West Virginia, Randolph went into politics and waged such a forceful campaign that he was elected, over an older and more experienced opponent, in a landslide.

Because of his success in influencing fellow representatives, President Franklin D. Roosevelt chose him to steer special wartime legislation through the house.

In a private popularity survey conducted by a group of Washington professional men, Roosevelt and Randolph were voted unanimously as the most charming personalities in government service at the time—but Randolph took the lead over the President in connection with his capacity to influence others with his boundless enthusiasm.

After 14 years in Congress, Randolph accepted one of the many offers he received from private industry.

He became assistant to the president of Capital Airlines, while the company was operating in the red, and within two years had helped with his matchless energy to lift it into first position as to earnings in the airline transportation field.

Speaking of Randolph's pleasing personality, the president of Capital Airlines recently said: "He more than earns his salary, not alone by the actual works he performs—but more especially for the enthusiasm he inspires among other members of the firm."

No one is "born enthusiastic." It is a trait that is acquired. You can acquire it, too.

"SELL" YOURSELF FIRST

Remember that in almost every contact with others you are trying, in a sense, to sell them something. That's true in all except trivial relationships. First convince yourself of the value of your idea, your product, your service—or yourself.

Examine it—or yourself—critically. Learn the flaws in whatever you are trying to sell—and eliminate or correct them. Be thoroughly convinced of the "rightness" of your product or idea.

Armed with this conviction, cultivate the habit of thinking positively, forcefully, energetically and you will find enthusiasm developing of itself—with the authoritative ring of true sincerity to help you project it to others.

The next column will tell you how your voice can help you achieve success.

VOICE OFT KEY TO CHARACTER

When Sam Jones, the great evangelist, was asked the secret of his ability to sway audiences with his sermons he replied, "It's not so much what I say as the way I say it." Your voice and manner of speaking can help you win success in life.

The most successful salesmen, politicians, lawyers, clergymen and educators are those who have learned the art of putting "something" into their voice tones that projects their own personalities and enthusiasm for their subjects.

William Jennings Bryan, scheduled to speak for 45 minutes at the Mormon Tabernacle in Salt Lake City, held his audience spellbound for two hours and 15 minutes—and his listeners applauded for more!

"I doubt if a dozen people could tell you the gist of his speech the next day," the head of the Mormon Church said. "It was the voice alone that captured and held the crowd."

A MARVELOUS INSTRUMENT

The human voice is a marvelous instrument through which the trained speaker can give his words far more emphasis and emotional appeal than their simple meanings convey. In its most superlative use, the voice can carry the same degree of impact as beautifully executed music.

Anyone can develop a strong, positive tone of voice with practice. And most public school systems offer adult speech classes, at low cost, where you can obtain professional help if necessary.

It is a lamentable fact that few people actually *know* how their voice sounds to others. The proximity of our ears to our own vocal organs distorts the sound. Therefore, it would pay you to make a tape recording of your voice and play it back to yourself. And it would help to ask your closest friend for constructive criticism of your voice tone, volume, and the degree of sincerity and enthusiasm you convey.

VOICE—NOT LANGUAGE

Remember that we are speaking of voice—not language. That's a subject that can fill volumes but which we will discuss in a later column.

Practice expressing your ideas clearly and confidently. Be an extrovert about it. Declaim to yourself before a mirror. Reading poetry or other literature aloud is also helpful. Put drama, excitement, enthusiasm into your voice when you read the bedtime story to the children—and watch them perk up with renewed interest!

The voice, like the eyes, is one of the "windows to the soul." It is one of the measures by which people judge you. Conversely, you can learn to size up others by their voices.

Almost any experienced trial lawyer can spot a lying witness by his hesitancy and weakness of tone. A storm of uncontrolled words reveals the loudmouth and bully. The skilled doctor detects the hypochondriac by his whining bid for sympathy. By making a game of it, you can soon learn far more about others through voices than they ever intend to reveal.

Remember that the people you meet along the road to success gain their first impression about you from your voice and your personal appearance. We will discuss the latter in our next column.

NEAT GROOMING
PAYS DIVIDENDS

Nothing succeeds like success—and success usually is attracted to the person who looks and acts successful. In my lifelong studies to determine why some people achieve immense wealth and fame while others are dismal failures I have found no greater truth than this: "Success requires no apologies, failure permits no alibis." Rightly or wrongly human nature is such that first impressions usually are the ones that endure. More important, the first impression may be the only one we have a chance to make. Therefore, it must be good!

SELF-CRITICISM DEMANDED

Anyone capable of reading this column is acquainted with the ordinary rules of personal cleanliness. But the fight for success demands a much higher, more self-critical order of grooming that pays special attention to details that are otherwise neglected. For example, do your fingernails pass close inspection? A manicure, given by wife or sister, costs nothing. Does your neckline have that "between trims" look? A quick run over with a safety razor will make it neat.

Anyone can shine his own shoes and press his own clothing to help himself present a good appearance at no cost.

But remember that you can make no better investment toward success than in buying good clothing, accessories and haberdashery. That doesn't mean that you should splurge all your capital in a buying spree, however. By watching for sales you can find genuine bargains at substantial savings. And women, of course, can fill out their wardrobes tremendously by taking one of the many free courses in sewing or dressmaking offered by YWCA's, public schools, and recreational groups.

WEAR SUNDAY "BEST"

For those who can possibly afford it, I earnestly suggest one complete "Sunday best" outfit of an exceptionally well-tailored suit or smartly designed dress for "first impression" use.

Again, rightly or wrongly you will find that people go far out of their way to help the person who looks affluent but shy away from those who look sorely in need! Granted that it's a flaw in human nature, it's one that must be taken into account.

There's another reason, perhaps even more important, why you need to keep yourself perfectly groomed, from the skin out, whenever you are in the public eye.

Good grooming will give you a psychological lift and

greater confidence in yourself. Your confidence will be even greater if you are accustomed to being well dressed. Nothing is more revealing than the ill-at-ease man who gives himself away by fidgeting with an unfamiliar cufflink or runs his finger around an unaccustomed collar.

WOMEN'S TRICK USEFUL

Many men, too, could well follow the trick women use to bolster their ego by buying a new—and possibly unneeded—hat. Whatever it is you need to give your mental attitude a boost—get it! A new hat, necktie, or pair of shoes can work wonders.

There are tricks of dress, too, that can help impress people. A new acquaintance may not remember your name— but he'll surely remember the man who wore the white carnation or the immense ring.

George S. May, Chicago business consultant and golf promoter, wears extravagantly designed sport shirts as a personal trademark that has helped lift him to great heights of fame and fortune.

Learn first, however, to dress appropriately to the occasion at hand and you'll be taking a long step toward your own success.

LEADERS MAKE
DECISIONS EASILY

Success comes more rapidly to those persons who can lead and supervise others. Despite popular misconception, leaders are made—not born. But they are self-made.

You—anyone—can be a leader. But only you can make yourself into one.

The most outstanding quality of leadership is willingness to make decisions.

The person who won't or can't make decisions—after he has sufficient facts on which to base them—can never supervise others.

You can train yourself to make decisions quickly and with a minimum of fretful worrying. It's a matter of habit. You can develop the good habit of deciding now, immediately, on a course of action or you can develop the bad habit of procrastination.

Learn, first of all, to distinguish between big and little

decisions—those which have highly important risks or consequences, and those where the outcome makes little difference.

Make little decisions as rapidly as possible. Give yourself more time on the big ones, to make sure you have all facts in hand and have related them carefully from the standpoint of logic. But set yourself a definite time limit—and when it expires, make your decision instantly.

And remember, once you've made a decision, never look back at it to wonder—or regret—what might have happened had you taken another course. Such contemplation is useless. It merely takes your mind off the new decisions that will inevitably be facing you.

By demonstrating a willingness—and eagerness, even—to make decisions, you will show others that you are willing to accept responsibility. Recognition of that fact will bring you the respect of others, particularly superiors. This world is so populated by buck-passers that they'll be pleasurably surprised to discover someone anxious to help shoulder responsibility by making decisions. Hence, you'll immediately be singling yourself out from the masses that shirk them.

By consciously trying to shorten the time it takes you to make a decision, you'll help yourself develop stronger initiative, better judgment, a more flexible attitude and open-mindedness.

In short, adopt an aggressive attitude toward decisions. Seek them out and make them! In doing so you'll find that often you've prevented little problems from becoming big ones.

If there's a decision to be made don't let it lie there and hope it'll go away.

It never will.

PROGRESS CALLS
FOR OPEN MINDS

An open mind is a free mind. The person who closes his mind to new ideas, concepts and people is locking a door that enslaves his own mentality. Intolerance is a two-edged scythe that on its backswing cuts off opportunities and lines of communication.

When you open your mind, you give your imagination freedom to act for you. You develop vision.

It's hard to realize now that less than six decades ago there were men who laughed at the Wright Brothers' experiments at flight. And barely three decades ago, Lindbergh could scarcely find backers for his Trans-Atlantic flight.

SCOFFERS SCORNED NOW

Today, men of vision freely predict man will soon fly to the moon—but no one's laughing. It's the scoffers who are held in scorn.

A closed mind is a sign of a static personality. It lets

progress pass it by and hence can never take advantage of the opportunities progress offers.

Only if you have an open mind can you grasp the full impact of the first rule of the Science of Success: "Whatever the mind of man can conceive and believe, the mind can achieve."

The man blessed with an open mind performs wonderful feats in business, industry and the professions while the man with the closed mind is still shouting "impossible."

TAKE STOCK OF SELF

It would be well for you to take stock of yourself. Are you among those who say "I can" and "It will be done" or do you fall in the group that says "Nobody can"—at the very moment somebody else is accomplishing it?

An open mind requires faith—in yourself, your fellow man and the Creator who laid out a pattern of progress for Man and his universe.

The days of superstition are gone. But the shadow of prejudice is as dark as ever. You can come out into the light by closely examining your own personality. Do you make decisions based on reason and logic rather than on emotion and preconceived ideas? Do you listen closely, attentively and thoughtfully to the other fellow's arguments? Do you seek for facts rather than hearsay and rumor?

FRESH THOUGHT NEEDED

The human mentality withers unless in constant contact with the stimulating influence of fresh thought. The Communists, in their brain-washing technique, know that the quickest way to break a man's will is to isolate his mind, cutting him off from the books, newspapers, radio and other normal channels of intellectual communication.

Under such circumstances, the intellect dies for lack of nourishment. Only the strongest will and the purest faith can save it.

Is it possible that you have imprisoned your mind in a social and cultural concentration camp? Have you subjected yourself to a brain-washing of your own making, isolating you from ideas that could lead to success?

If so, it's time to sweep aside the bars of prejudice that imprison your intellect.

Open your mind and set it free!

ATTAIN YOUR GOAL
WITH SINCERITY

To achieve success, you must have a definite major goal in life. Your chances of attaining that goal will be infinitely greater if it includes a wish to provide others with a better product or services. The operative word in the sentence is "sincere." Sincerity is a trait that pays off in self-satisfaction, self-respect, and the spiritual security of a clear conscience.

We have to live with ourselves 24 hours a day. The partnership may not be pleasant if we don't conduct ourselves so we have the fullest respect for that invisible "other self" who can guide us to glory, fame and riches—or relegate us to misery and failure.

ABE ANECDOTE

A friend of Abraham Lincoln once told him that his enemies were saying terrible things about him. "I don't care what they say," exclaimed Lincoln, "so long as they're not telling the truth."

Sincerity of purpose made Lincoln immune against fear of criticism. And the same trait helped him meet seemingly insurmountable problems growing out of the War Between the States.

Sincerity is a matter of motive. Therefore, it's something that others have a right to question before granting you their time, energy or money.

TEST YOURSELF

Before embarking on a course of action, test your sincerity yourself. Ask yourself this question: "Granted that I seek personal gain in what I am about to do, am I giving fair value in service or goods for the profit or wages I hope to make—or am I hoping to get something for nothing?"

Sincerity is one of the hardest things to prove to others. But you must be prepared—and eager—to do so.

Here's how one person did it.

Martha Berry founded a school for mountain boys and girls of North Georgia whose parents couldn't pay for their schooling.

Needing money to carry on her work, she went to Henry Ford and asked for a modest donation. Ford refused.

UNIQUE REQUEST

"Well then," said Miss Berry, "will you give us a bushel of peanuts?"

The novel request amused Ford so much he gave her the money for the peanuts.

Miss Berry had her youngsters plant and replant them until their sales piled up a fund of $500. Then she took the money back to Ford and showed him how she had multiplied his small donation.

Ford was so impressed that he made her a gift of enough tractors and other farm equipment to put her school farm on a self-supporting basis. Moreover, he gave her through the years more than $1,000,000 for the beautiful stone buildings which now stand on the campus of the school Miss Berry founded.

"I couldn't help being impressed," he said, "with her sincerity and the marvelous way she applied it in behalf of needy boys and girls."

You can help achieve your own goal in life by such dramatic proof of your sincere desire to help others.

HUMILITY AIDS IN ACHIEVEMENT

Many people think of humility, one of the principal ingredients of a pleasing personality, as a negative virtue. But it isn't. It's a powerfully positive one.

Humility actually is a force that Man can put into operation for his own good.

All of his greatest advances—spiritual, cultural or material—have been based on it.

It is the prime requisite of true Christianity. With its help Gandhi set India free. And again with its help, Dr. Albert Schweitzer is creating a better world for thousands of Africans—for all of us—in the jungles.

Humility is an absolute essential to the type of personality you need to achieve personal success, no matter what your goal. And you will find it even more essential after you have reached the top.

Without humility you will never gain wisdom; for one of the most important traits of a wise man is the ability to acknowledge "I was wrong."

Hence, without humility you will never be able to find what I call the "seed of equivalent benefit" in adversity and defeat.

Every adversity or defeat, I have found, carries with it something to help you overcome it—and even rise above it. Let me give you an example:

R.G. LeTourneau started in business as a garage operator, failed at that, and went into the contracting business.

Again financial disaster struck. He was a sub-contractor on the Hoover Dam project when he ran into an unexpected stratus of very hard stone. He lost everything he owned.

COMFORT IN PRAYER

LeTourneau didn't try to blame others or the forces of nature for his losses. He took responsibility himself. After each setback he found comfort in prayer.

It was while praying for guidance that he found the "seed of equivalent benefit" from his last defeat. He'd go into the business of manufacturing machines which could move any kind of earth or rock—including the type that licked him at Hoover Dam!

As a result, LeTourneau earth-moving machinery is now in use throughout the world. LeTourneau has four plants turning them out and his personal fortune runs into millions.

GIVE TO CHURCHES

But the story of his humility doesn't stop there.

To express gratitude for the help he received in turning defeat to victory, LeTourneau now gives most of his income to churches and devotes a large portion of his time to lay preaching.

Sometimes, humility turns defeat into spiritual blessing.

In 1955, I arrived as a house-guest of Lee Braxton, businessman and former mayor of Whiteville, N.C., on the very day he discovered he had suffered a heavy financial loss due to the negligence of an associate he had trusted implicitly for years.

"How many successful businesses have you built and managed?" I asked.

"About 15 in all," Braxton said, "including the First National Bank of Whitesville. I never lost a penny in any of them. That's why this hurts. It's an ugly jab at my pride."

STRENGTH IN FAILURE

"That's good," I told him. "You are about to learn that you have as much strength in times of failure as when you are succeeding. Your loss has been a great blessing if it leaves you gifted with humility of the heart and gratitude for those riches you still possess. With it, you can be more successful than ever."

Braxton's face lighted up with a broad smile.

"That's right," he said. "I hadn't thought of it that way."

A few months later, I received a letter from Braxton. He said his income has climbed to an all-time high, more than making up the loss he suffered.

Humility is a positive force that knows no limitations.

SENSE OF HUMOR
WILL EASE WAY

Your sense of humor is a tremendous asset that can smooth the bumps on the road to success. If you are one of those blessed with a naturally cheerful disposition you can count yourself lucky. If not, however, you can develop one.

It's obvious that a good sense of humor makes you a more likable, more attractive personality. That alone will help you achieve success.

But more than that, it can help you overcome momentary failures, to rise above them and seek out new courses of action that will put you back on the success beam.

A keen sense of humor is based chiefly on humility. With its help we can recognize our failings and fears, laugh at them, and surmount them. And also, with its aid you can push aside the worries of adverse circumstances so that they can't become obstacles on the pathway to your goal.

FAMILY HELPED

It was exactly this type of constant good humor that permitted Minnie Lee Steen and her four small children to endure severe hardships in the Utah deserts while her husband, Charles, hunted for the uranium he was certain was there in 1950.

Water was so scarce the baby had to drink sweetened tea. The family was so low on food they had to rely on venison for meat. Store bread was such a luxury the kids "bolted it like cake."

Through all this, Charles and Minnie Lee Steen kept their sense of humor for two years. For the children, they made a game of their troubles—a game of "pioneer" they enjoyed hugely. As a result, their troubles never had a chance to crush the doughty family.

In the end, Steen won. He struck uranium on a claim that in three years produced $70,000,000 worth of ore. His holdings are estimated at a minimum of $60,000,000.

SOUGHT A HANDICAP

Charles and Minnie Lee Steen are sitting on top of the world now, largely because of their persistent good humor.

And it was the same type of good humor that helped Jonas Mayer when he came out of World War I with a shattered jaw, a game leg and, for all practical purposes, no hearing.

He deliberately sought a field where deafness would be

a handicap—selling—and also won. Today he is vice-president of the American Linen Supply Co., Chicago.

"Without a sense of humor," says Joe Mayer, "you can't have any fun.

"And the more you learn to laugh at your problems, the less important they appear until, finally, they don't exist at all."

COUNT BLESSINGS

What Joe Mayer, Charles Steen and thousands of others have done, you can also do.

Learn first of all to count your blessings and assets more often than you do your troubles and problems. Put them uppermost in your mind. If you have difficulty doing this, make a written inventory of them and read them over to yourself whenever you start worrying.

Remember that many of your blessings are hidden treasures, commonplace everyday items or qualities that you simply take for granted. Your health, for example. Or the love, admiration and faith your family has in you.

Learn to regard your problems as stepping-stones to success. Each one you overcome brings you closer to your goal.

COULD BE WORSE

Remember that every bad situation could be worse—like the man who cursed his luck because he had no shoes, until he met a man who had no feet. Never let a day go by without a prayer of thanks for the bounty you enjoy, no matter how small it is. And go out of your way every day to expend a part of your time and energy to helping others. You'll be casting bread upon the waters.

Remember too that no problem is unique or new. You can always seek advice or help. And you are never alone. A Greater Power is with you always. Learn to rely on it. Make it a policy to meet your problems head-on, in a spirit of audacity, courage, and decisiveness. For as Emerson said:

"An adventure is nothing more than an inconvenience, rightly considered."

AMERICANS HELD
TOO IMPATIENT

Americans are in a hurry. Foreigners regard this as our most singular characteristic. And they're right. It's a national trait arising from the questing, forceful energy that is our greatest source of strength.

But this same energy—this driving force that demands immediate outlet in action—can also be a source of weakness. For it has made us the most impatient people in the world.

In wartime, many of our soldiers found themselves at fatal disadvantage to an enemy due to their typically American impatience. Frequently, they exposed themselves to fire unnecessarily instead of trying to out-wait a sniper.

PATIENCE DEMANDS COURAGE

Patience demands its own peculiar kind of courage. It's a persistent type of forbearance and fortitude that results from complete dedication to an ideal or goal. Therefore, the more strongly you are imbued with the idea of achieving your principal goal in life, the more patience you will have to overcome obstacles.

The sort of patience I'm talking about is dynamic, rather than passive. It's a positive force rather than an acquiescent submission to circumstances. And it springs from the same type of immense energy that we Americans possess in such abundance. However, it is closely controlled and tightly channeled toward a single goal with almost fanatical fixation.

It's the kind of patience Thomas A. Edison possessed when he was searching for a suitable material as a filament for the incandescent lamp.

DEFEATED 10,000 TIMES

By count, Edison suffered 10,000 defeats as he tried and discarded one material after another until he finally found the right one.

Once I asked Edison during a conversation what he would have done had he still been unsuccessful.

"In that case, I'd still be in my laboratory looking for the right answer instead of wasting my time talking to you," he answered with a smile that softened the words.

Constance Bannister considers impatience her greatest fault. Yet she deliberately went into a profession where patience is the greatest prerequisite—photographing babies— and became the most successful person in the field.

"With a baby, to get the expression you want, you must

repeat and repeat, explain and explain, in a soothing mono-tone voice," she says.

DEVELOPS SENSE OF HUMOR

"I like photographing babies because it helps me so much. It develops my sense of humor and helps me to be creative in other fields."

How can you develop patience? It's easy, provided you have reached a decision as to your major definite goal in life and concentrate on it with all your will until you are filled with a burning desire to achieve it—and your every thought, action and prayer is directed toward that end.

It was exactly this same sort of fixed idea that provided the patience necessary for Edison to invent the electric light, for Salk to produce a vaccine against polio, for Hilary to climb Mount Everest, and for Helen Keller to triumph over seemingly insurmountable physical handicaps.

The same sort of concentration on your major goal will provide the patience you need to achieve it.

THERE'S WISDOM
IN SHOWMANSHIP

In today's lesson on the Science of Success, let's consider the case of Joe Dull. Joe's a hard-working guy—diligent, faithful, punctual, dependable and resourceful. He gives the boss more than his due in time, effort and energy. Surely, you'd think, Joe is bound to achieve success.

But he isn't. Joe isn't going anywhere. Others, considerably less worthy, are getting the promotion and raises.

The fact is that Joe lacks showmanship. He simply never attracts the boss's attention.

Are you like Joe? If so, develop showmanship and watch how much easier it is to climb the ladder of success.

But a word of caution is necessary. There's a distinct difference between true showmanship and some less honest ways of attracting attention to yourself. Apple-polishing, for example, will gain you more enemies than friends. So will outright boastfulness.

True showmanship is something creative. It has, as the name implies, a certain entertainment value. It demands ingenuity and a nice sense of timing.

A CANDIDATE'S EXAMPLE

I remember, for example, when Alexander Brummit was running for sheriff of Wise County, Virginia.

Brummit organized a "working bee" to build a new home for a widowed mother. He visited citizens and got them to join the work force and induced merchants and stores to contribute the materials and furnishings. He even arranged for the volunteer workers' wives to prepare a big picnic feast.

After the house was erected, in a single day, Brummit turned the picnic that evening into a political rally, delivering a speech in the ready-made throng that included almost every voting-age citizen of the county.

He thanked them for joining with him to do a fine thing for an individual member of the community and concluded by asking their help again—for the community as a whole— "by electing me to office to give the people of Wise County the kind of law enforcement they deserve."

His showmanship put him into office by a landslide.

MACFADDEN WAS SHOWMAN

Bernarr Macfadden's flair for showmanship sometimes bordered on the bizarre, but he made it pay off in millions by parachuting in red flannel underwear from airplanes, by walking down Broadway in his bare feet, and by displaying his extraordinary muscular development.

You needn't go to such extremes. Sometimes special attention to the niceties of courtesy and politeness can achieve the same purpose.

Glenn R. Fouche, president of the Stayform Co., tells the story of a friend who rose to president of a large hoist and derrick company in Texas by that simple method.

As a young salesman, when he sold his first small hoist, he wrote the head of the shipping department thanking him for getting the order delivered promptly. He wrote the paint department superintendent to tell how proud he was when he saw the bright red finish as the hoist was unpacked. Through the years he made a point of trying to let each member of the firm know how worthwhile he thought their services were.

Remember that true showmanship must follow a positive course. It never "knocks down" or minimizes the value of other people. No one can climb to success on someone else's shoulder.

If you are like good old dependable Joe Dull, you may be too modest, too shy and retiring, to present your ideas, suggestions and offers of extra service to the boss in person. In that case, use written memos. They also insure that credit goes where it is due!

But don't wait. Start now to use showmanship as a tool to build your success!

HOPES, DREAMS
BRING GREATNESS

Hope is the raw material with which you build success. Hope crystallizes into faith, faith into determination and determination into action.

It springs principally from your dreams of a better world, a better life, a better tomorrow.

On the basis of hope, you will decide upon your definite major goal in life and translate it into actuality.

Years ago, for example, James J. Hill was sitting at a telegraph key sending the message of a woman to a friend whose husband had been killed in a railroad wreck. The message said "Your grief can be softened by your hope of meeting your husband in a better world."

"HOPE" BROUGHT DREAM

The word "hope" stuck in Hill's mind. He began thinking about the powers and possibilities of hope. That led him to dream of someday building a new railroad to the West.

The dream gradually strengthened into a clear-cut determination which Hill carried to fruition by building the Great Northern Railway system.

Manuel L. Quezon dared to dream and hope of self-government for his beloved islands, the Philippines. He even dared to hope that he might someday be President of a free Philippine republic.

WORKED FOR 24 YEARS

His hope became faith—and then action, as he maneuvered to get himself appointed resident commissioner of the islands.

For 24 years, he bent every effort toward the day when the territory would become a separate country. I know, because he was my good friend and he let me advise him frequently on ways to achieve his political aims.

His efforts, as everyone knows, were successful. On the day he was elected President of the new Philippine republic, Quezon sent me this telegram:

"May I thank you from the fullness of my heart for having inspired me to keep the fires of hope burning in my heart until this glorious day of triumph."

DREAM BIG DREAMS

The lesson for you in Quezon's story is that you must give your imagination free play to create hope. Dare to dream big dreams. Fill yourself with the faith that nothing is impossible for "whatever the mind of man can conceive and believe, the mind of man can achieve."

From your hope and faith, decide on a definite major goal. Write it down. Commit it to memory. Make it the fixed star on which you chart your course to success. Then take action to make it come true.

Every success story with a happy ending starts with the words: "Once upon a time there was a man who hoped that someday . . ."

Yours must start out the same way.

OTHERS MEASURE
YOU BY SPEECH

Every new person you meet is a judge. You are the defendant. Each tries, consciously or unconsciously—on even the most casual acquaintance—to judge what sort of person you are, how you think, what makes you tick.

What these persons think of you during such brief encounters will depend on two things—how you look and how you speak.

You must make the best impression possible in every instance. For the very next person you meet may be the one who can give you a tremendous boost up the ladder to success.

Your manner of speaking and choice of words will carry far more weight for or against you than any other factor.

Therefore, you should make this a rule for life: Always choose your words with the same thought and carefulness you would exercise if you were speaking in a stadium before 10,000 persons with your words being carried to 10,000,000 more by radio.

SIMPLICITY IS BEST

That doesn't mean that you must use high-flown, formal or stilted language. Simple, conversational English will carry far more force and meaning.

And while grammatical correctness is highly desirable, some of the most profound thoughts have been expressed ungrammatically, as in the case of Einstein.

But an absolute essential is a good vocabulary. For almost invariably we think in terms of words. And without a goodly store of them our range of thought is narrowly limited.

If you lack a good vocabulary, make a daily habit of browsing through a good dictionary. Study Roget's Thesaurus for the shades of meaning between synonyms.

Learn one new word each day, writing it down in at least 10 sentences for practice. Go out of your way to use it as frequently as possible.

PACKED WITH MEANING

The word may not be long or difficult, but it should be packed with meaning. Concentrate on the verbs and those words carrying subjective ideas that are hard to express unless you have the right word at your fingertips.

Then learn to use the right word in the right place at the right time. This comes only from practice in everyday conversation.

As of this moment, erase completely from your vocabulary all profanity, blasphemy, obscenity or irreverence.

The use of profanity or blasphemy is a dead giveaway that one lacks the word-power to express his emotions properly.

Obscenity, off-color jokes and the double entendre are resorted to only by the boor who lacks the cleverness to be really funny or amusing.

Irreverence to one's own Deity or that of others is always in unforgivably bad taste.

This discussion on the use of appropriate words calls to mind a story I once heard about a grand dinner given by a former prime minister of Britain.

COCKNEY CRASHER

One very distinguished-looking gentleman showed up in impeccably correct attire. His appearance impressed everyone. But no one seemed to know him.

As dinner was served, a waiter offered the well-dressed stranger a platter of baked potatoes. The guest smiled broadly and spoke for the first time.

"Ah! Them's the pups for me!" he proclaimed in a raucous Cockney accent.

He was ejected instantly as a party-crasher.

The moral of the story is: If you don't know the right word for the occasion, keep your mouth shut and you'll stay clear of trouble.

BE OPTIMISTIC TO ATTAIN GOAL

Optimism is a matter of mental habit. You can learn to practice the habit of optimism—and thereby greatly enhance your chances of achieving success. Or you can drive yourself into the pit of pessimism and failure.

Optimism is one of the most important traits of a pleasing personality. But it results largely from other traits we have discussed—a good sense of humor, hopefulness, the ability to overcome fear, contentment, a positive mental attitude, flexibility, faith and decisiveness.

The pessimist fears the Devil and spends most of his time fighting him.

The optimist loves his Creator and spends his time worshipping Him.

You can fight pessimism through complete belief in two of the most basic truths of the Science of Success:

1. "Whatever the mind of Man can conceive and believe, the mind can achieve."
2. "Every adversity and defeat carries the seed of an equivalent benefit, if we are ingenious enough to find it."

LAY PLEASANT PLANS

Instead of worrying about the bad things that might befall you, spend a few minutes every day enumerating the pleasant events that will happen tomorrow, next week, next year! By thinking about them, you will find yourself laying plans to make them happen! Then you are getting the habit of optimism.

Remember that no great leader or successful man was ever a pessimist. What could such a leader promise his followers but despair and defeat?

Even in the darkest days of the Civil War, leaders on both sides—such as Lincoln and Lee—held faith in better days to come.

Franklin D. Roosevelt's natural optimism breathed a new spirit of hope into a dejected nation in the depths of the Depression.

Even infamous leaders—the Hitlers, Stalins, Mussolinis and Maos—rely on the promise of better days to win followers with such catch phrases as "tomorrow the world," "nothing to lose but your chains," and "the new Asia."

Can you—living under the finest social, economic and political system in human history—afford to have any less?

Remember that like attracts like in human relations, no matter what the rule may be in the physical world. An optimist tends to congregate with optimists, just as success attracts more success.

But the pessimist breeds worries and trouble without

speaking a word or performing an act because his negative mental attitude serves as a perfect magnet for them.

Optimism is, in itself, a kind of success. For it means you have a healthy, peaceful and contented mind. An exceedingly wealthy man can be a failure physically, if his constant pessimism has brought him a case of ulcers.

Optimism isn't a state of mind in which you throw judgment to the winds in starry-eyed belief future events will take care of themselves. Such an outlook is only for fools.

USE SOUND JUDGMENT

It is, however, a firm belief that you can make things come out right by thinking ahead and deciding on a course of action based on sound judgment. Let me give an example.

At the height of the big boom of 1928, there were those false optimists who refused to believe that the bubble could ever burst. They jeered those few farsighted "pessimists" who warned that the nation was treading on dangerously inflationary and speculative ground.

When the bottom dropped out, the "optimists" were caught short. Many lacked the spiritual strength to seek victory in defeat and revealed themselves as the true pessimists.

But those who had looked ahead fearlessly and honestly had put themselves in position by selling stock short and other devices—to make a killing. They were revealed as the true optimists.

You can be that kind of optimist. Learn to meet the future head-on. Analyze it. Weigh the factors with clear judgment. Then decide upon your course of action to make things turn out the way you want them.

You'll find that the future holds nothing that you ever need fear.

Part Three

SCIENCE OF SUCCESS SERIES, SEPTEMBER 1956– JANUARY 1957

"The rapid pace at which the world is moving today has created thousands of needs which did not even exist fifty years ago. This formula will prove that one's only limitation is that which he sets up in his own mind."

Article I

SUCCESS FOR YOU

Your success is unlimited except by your own ambition and desires! If *you* are ready, you can mark this day as the most important turning point of your life regardless of your past failures, your present handicaps, or what it is that you desire most from life.

There is a formula for success—just as there is a formula for failure. The seventeen-part formula is being made available to readers, one each week through this column. This formula has been used in whole or at least in part by every human being who has ever achieved any measure of success.

W. Clement Stone used the success formula so effectively that he is now president of four large insurance companies, although he began business with only $100 in cash and the formula!

Earl Nightingale, the famous radio and television star of Chicago, came into possession of the formula only a few years ago while working on a modest salary. He used it so effectively that he is now president of two corporations and a director of several others.

Brownie Wise, a former housewife who is now one of the most successful business women in the world, came into possession of the famous formula only a few years ago. Today she is the head of Tupperware Home Parties, with a nation-wide organization of many thousands of employees.

Conrad Hilton was born in humble circumstances in a plain adobe house in Cisco, Texas. By applying only a portion of the seventeen parts of the success formula he has become the head of the largest system of hotels in the world. He recently said, "Your value is determined by what you make of yourself."

It makes but little difference where a man begins in this country. The important thing is—what is his goal, and how does he plan to attain it?

Where else but in the U.S.A. could a humble immigrant start out by pushing a banana cart and wind up as the head of the largest banking system of the world, as Italian-born Gianini did? He not only lifted himself from poverty to riches by use of the success formula, but that same formula made the Bank of America, which he founded, the largest banking system of the world.

We are living during a time which has been blessed with more inventions and more ways to market personal services than have existed in the history of mankind, prior to the beginning of this century.

Don't let anyone discourage you by suggesting that opportunities are a thing of the past. The rapid pace at which the world is moving today has created thousands of needs which did not even exist fifty years ago. This formula will prove that one's only limitation is that which he sets up in his own mind.

The very first step one must take to success will appear in this column next week.

Article II

CHOOSE YOUR GOAL

Before beginning to build a home, one first evolves a satisfactory house plan. And you wouldn't start on a trip without knowing where you are going or how you intended to get there.

But only about two people out of every thousand know precisely what they desire from life, and have workable plans for attaining their goals. These are the men and women who are leaders in every walk of life—the big successes who have made life pay off on their own terms.

And the strangest thing about these successful people is that they have no more personality, no more education, and no more opportunities than others who never make the grade.

If you know exactly what you want, and have absolute faith in your ability to get it, you can achieve success. If you are *not* sure what you want from life, start now to find out.

First, write out a clear statement of what you desire

most—the one thing or circumstance which, after you attain it, would justify your calling yourself a success.

Second, write out a clear outline of the plan by which you intend to attain this objective, and clearly state in your plan what you intend to give, in return.

Third, set a definite time limit within which you intend to acquire the object of your definite major purpose.

Fourth, memorize what you have written and repeat it many times daily as a prayer. End the prayer by expressing gratitude for having received that for which your plan calls.

Follow these instructions to the letter, and you will be amazed at how soon your entire life will change for the better. Keep this procedure to yourself lest you become disturbed by the skeptics near you who may not understand the profound law you are following.

Remember—*nothing ever "just happens!"* You have to *make things happen*, including individual success. Success in every calling is the result of definite action, carefully planned, and persistently carried out.

Definiteness of purpose makes the word "impossible" obsolete. It is the starting-point of all successful achievements. It is available to you and everyone, without money and without price. All you need is the personal initiative to embrace it and use it.

Unless you know what you want from life, and are determined to get it, you will be forced to accept the mere crumbs left by others who knew where they were going and had a plan for getting there.

To be sure of success, saturate your mind completely with your goal. Think and plan about that which you desire. *Keep your mind off that which you do not want.* You have here the practical formula which all successful people follow.

Article III

MAINTAIN A POSITIVE
MENTAL ATTITUDE

When asked what had contributed most to his success, the late Henry Ford said, "I keep my mind so busy thinking about what I wish to accomplish that there is no room in it for thinking about things I don't want." When asked what he needed most in the successful operation of his great automobile empire, Ford promptly exclaimed, "More men who don't know anything about how something can't be done."

And Thomas Edison, the greatest inventor of all times, shocked his friends by stating that his deafness was his greatest blessing because it saved him from the trouble of having to listen to negative circumstances in which he had no interest, and enabled him to concentrate on his aims and purposes in a positive mental attitude.

One of man's strangest traits lies in the fact that it often takes tragedy, failure, or some form of misfortune to make him realize the power of a positive mental attitude.

Milo C. Jones of Fort Atkinson, Wisconsin, made only a modest living as a farmer—until he was stricken down by paralysis. Then he discovered that his mind power was greater than brawn and muscle power. His idea for "Little Pig" sausages made him fabulously rich on the same farm which previously had yielded only a living.

Your mental attitude is the medium by which you can balance your life and your relationship to people and circumstances, to attract what you desire. "Whatever your mind can conceive and believe, your mind can achieve." Clip out this line and paste it on your mirror where you can see it every day of your life.

Article IV

GO THE EXTRA MILE

A nd whosoever shall compel thee to go a mile, go with him twain." This may well be the most profound teaching of Scriptures. It goes far beyond the Golden Rule, admonishing one to give his fellow men not only what they expect and have a right to receive—but far more.

The concept of the "extra mile" is presented in another part of the Scriptures which states, "Whatsoever a man soweth that shall he also reap."

Going the extra mile means rendering more and better service than customary or necessary—and doing it in a positive, pleasing mental attitude. It is the only just reason for anyone to request an increase in pay, a promotion, or any favor whatsoever.

Carol Downes, a young bank teller, changed positions and went to work for William C. Durant, founder of the great General Motors Corporation. The first day something happened which gave Downes one promotion after another and made him a very rich man.

When the quitting bell rang, everyone in the place rushed for the door. Downes remained at his desk. A few minutes later, Durant came out of his office, saw Downes still at his desk, and requested that he bring him a pencil.

Downes got two new pencils, carefully sharpened them, and smilingly handed them to the motor tycoon. Each evening Downes stayed long after quitting time, hoping, as he said, to be available when his chief wanted something. That mental attitude brought Downes a $50,000-a-year job through his association with Durant.

The benefits one receives from the habit of going the extra mile do not always come from the persons or the source to which the service is rendered. Sometimes the returns seem unduly delayed. But when they do come, they often are greatly multiplied by comparison with the nature and extent of the service rendered.

A wise man knows that before he can reap a harvest of riches of any sort, he must have first sown the proper seed of service entitling him to the harvest.

Article V

THINK ACCURATELY

Your power of thought is the only thing over which you have absolute control. To use this power effectively, you must think accurately. The sacred nature of this exclusive privilege is signified by the fact that the Creator reserved it for man as a marker which distinguishes him from all other living creatures.

Accurate thinkers permit no one to do their thinking for them. Successful people have a definite system by which they reach decisions with accuracy. They gather information and get the opinions of others. But in the final analysis they reserve for themselves the privilege of making decisions.

Accurate thinking is based upon two major fundamentals, (1) inductive reasoning based on assumption of unknown facts or hypotheses, when the facts are not available, and (2) deductive reasoning, based on known facts, or what are believed to be facts.

The accurate thinker always takes two important steps. First, he separates facts from fiction or hearsay evidence which cannot be verified. Second, he separates facts into two classes—important and unimportant.

An important fact is one which can be used to advantage in attaining your objective. All others are worthless.

It is a tragedy that many people base their thinking on irrelevant hearsay evidence and unimportant facts which lead only to misery and failure.

The accurate thinker recognizes that most "opinions" expressed by others are worthless, even dangerous if accepted as accurate, because they are based upon bias, prejudice, intolerance, egotism, fear and guess-work.

An accurate thinker turns a deaf ear to the person who begins a conversation with that hackneyed expression "*they say*" because he knows what he is about to hear will be nothing but loose talk.

EMOTIONS UNRELIABLE

The accurate thinker knows that no one has a right to express an opinion on any subject unless it is based on dependable facts. This rule would eliminate as worthless much of the so-called thinking of a vast majority of the people.

The accurate thinker recognizes that free "advice"— volunteered by friends and others—usually is not worthy of consideration. If he wants advice he seeks a dependable source and pays for it in one way or another. He knows that nothing of value is obtained without a consideration.

The accurate thinker knows that his emotions are not always reliable. He protects himself against their possible wrong influence by carefully examining and weighing them through his power of reason and the rules of logic.

James B. Duke had no formal schooling and never learned to write, but he developed a keen sense of accuracy in his thinking which made him one of the richest men in the world. He didn't waste time debating with himself over trivialities or unimportant facts. He reached decisions quickly after he had the facts.

One day he met an old friend who was shocked to hear that Duke planned to open two thousand tobacco stores. "My partner and I," said the friend, "have enough trouble with just two stores and you're thinking of opening two thousand. It's a mistake, Duke." "A mistake!" Duke exclaimed. "I've made mistakes all my life, and if there's one thing that has helped me it's the fact that when I make one I never stop to talk about it. I just go ahead and make some more."

SOME OF THEM RIGHT

So Duke went ahead with his chain of retail tobacco stores, which eventually did a weekly business of two million dollars. He left several million dollars to build Duke University, and that was only a small fraction of the wealth he accumulated by his quick, accurate decisions, some of which were right.

Elbert Hubbard has defined an executive as "a man who makes a lot of decisions and some of them are right."

Obviously, accurate thinking calls for the highest order

of self-discipline, a subject so closely related to accurate thinking that it will be presented in our next column.

Prompt and accurate decisions are the two most important foundation stones of success in all walks of life. They are not attainable without courageous and honest discipline of one's self.

Article VI

EXERCISE SELF-DISCIPLINE

The number one cause of individual failures is inability to get along harmoniously with people. In most instances this results from failure to discipline one's self.

Andrew Carnegie once said, "The man who cannot or will not exercise discipline over himself must submit to discipline by others." And again he said: "I have always made it a part of my business philosophy to caution my associates against the dangers of indiscreet use of authority and personal power, especially those who, through promotions, have but recently come into the possession of authority.

"Newly acquired power is something like newly acquired riches; it needs watching closely lest a man become the victim of his own power by its misuse. Here is where self-discipline gives a good account of itself. If a man has his own thoughts and actions under control, he makes these serve others in a manner which does not antagonize, but rather attracts friendly cooperation."

Thomas A. Edison tried out more than ten thousand

different ideas before he perfected the incandescent electric lamp. But he had the self-discipline to sustain him through all those defeats to victory. His self-discipline ushered in the great electrical age which transformed the entire mechanical and industrial world and made jobs for countless millions.

SELF-DISCIPLINE NEEDED

Self-discipline is the only sure means of developing and maintaining a positive mental attitude. It is the medium by which one learns from his mistakes and discovers the seed of an equivalent benefit in all of his failures and defeats.

You have in your mind-power everything you need to take you from where you are to where you desire to be in life. But the power consists of both a positive and a negative potentiality, and self-discipline, alone, can help you direct it to successful ends.

Self-discipline is an essential for the maintenance of sound health. And it is the means by which one concentrates his mind on that which he wants from life and keeps it from attracting that which he does not want through fear and worry.

Through self-discipline of almost unbelievable endurance Mahatma Gandhi freed India from the rule of the British without violence, without military organization and without money—a feat seldom achieved in the history of mankind.

Because he lacked self-discipline, Hitler destroyed his

country, caused the useless death of untold numbers of men, and lost his own life.

HE WON SUCCESS

Arthur Rubloff, well-known Chicago realtor, is now head of a $40,000,000 business. Through self-discipline he was able to raise himself from a shoe shine boy to his present prominent position. He conceived the idea of calling on three realty prospects a day—rain, shine, snow, or sleet. This took a lot of hours and a lot of foot-work. It also left him little time for any leisure. But Rubloff kept working his plan through the years, and it brought success. He couldn't have accomplished even part of this without strictly disciplining himself.

Henry Garfinkle of New York started out as a 13-year-old newsboy selling papers to passengers on the Staten Island Ferry. Through self-discipline, he overcame adversities and soon owned a concession inside the ferry terminal. Gradually he expanded and gained a reputation as an expert on circulation problems.

As a result, when a group of business men were trying to restore the financially sick firm of Greater Boston Distributors, Inc., they called on Garfinkle as their troubleshooter. His reputation grew from this experience and he became known as a circulation expert.

Gradually he began buying stock in the gigantic American News Co. and its subsidiary, Union News Co. This year he and a group of close associates won control of the two firms and Garfinkle was elected president. Self-discipline had paid off in a big way!

SILENCE IS PRECIOUS

Self-discipline makes it possible to turn on more will power and keep on instead of quitting when the going is hard and failure seems just around the corner.

There are two times in a man's life when he needs highly refined self-discipline to save him from ruin. One is when he is overtaken by failure or defeat, and the other is when he begins to rise to the higher levels of success.

Lastly, self-discipline teaches a man silence often is more appropriate and gives one more advantages than spoken words inspired by anger, hatred, jealousy, greed, intolerance or fear. And it is the means by which one develops and maintains that priceless habit of thinking about the possible effects of his words before he speaks.

UNBEATABLE MASTER MIND:
MASTER MIND ALLIANCE WINS

Two or more persons, actively engaged in pursuit of a definite purpose in a positive mental attitude, constitute an unbeatable force!

The Master Mind principle is the medium through which one may procure the full benefits of the experience, training, education, specialized knowledge and influence of others, as completely as if their minds were one's own.

When Andrew Carnegie was asked the secret of his success in the steel industry, he replied, "Personally I know nothing about the technicalities of making steel, but I have a Master Mind alliance with men who have the required knowledge."

HENRY FORD'S SECRET

His personal duties in the alliance were, he said, "To keep my associates actively engaged in a spirit of perfect harmony." He stressed that coordination of effort, known as cooperation, is not the same as the Master Mind because it need not be based on perfect harmony.

The Master Mind alliance between Mr. and Mrs. Henry Ford was the real secret of Ford's success. When Ford was struggling to build the first model of his automobile, he asked a local foundryman to cast thirty dollars' worth of parts and wait for the money until the end of the month. The foundryman refused. When Mrs. Ford heard about it, she persuaded her husband to "borrow" the money from a small savings account they held jointly, which he did under protest. Because of their Master Mind alliance, the giant Ford company came into being.

Perhaps the greatest Master Mind alliance in history existed between the Nazarene and His disciples. And tragedy struck when one of the allies betrayed Him just as it still strikes in any business, professional or marriage relationship when one member of the alliance becomes negative and breaks the condition of perfect harmony.

The most important document ever penned, the Declaration of Independence, was signed by fifty-six courageous men in a Master Mind alliance.

The Arthur Murrays, who operate a chain of dancing studios across the nation, are a marvelous example of the power of the Master Mind in action. The same is true of movie and television stars Roy Rogers and Dale Evans. Through a harmonious spiritual Master Mind relationship, Mr. and Mrs. Rogers overcame a deep personal tragedy and brought hope to thousands. When death claimed their mentally retarded baby daughter, Dale and Roy turned their grief into help for many other handicapped children.

WORKING IN HARMONY

The President of the United States and his Cabinet constitute one of the world's greatest and most powerful Master Mind alliances. The working relationship between our Federal Government and the states is another example of power through Master Mind alliance.

All human achievements above the level of mediocrity are the results of working together in a spirit of harmony—the Master Mind principle.

Lee S. Mytinger and Dr. William S. Casselberry of Long Beach, California, formed a Master Mind alliance some ten years ago to distribute a food supplement known as Nutrilite. They extended their Master Mind alliance until it now includes many thousands of Nutrilite distributors. Their annual sales are around $30,000,000, and it all started with practically no capital.

You, too, can achieve success through a Master Mind alliance. By allying yourself with at least one other person in a spirit of perfect harmony to achieve a common goal, you can attain heights difficult to reach alone.

Article VIII

HAVE FAITH IN YOURSELF:
USE THE UNBEATABLE MASTER—
WE DRAW POWER FROM
INNER WELL

In a one-room cabin in Kentucky, a small boy was lying on the hearth, learning to write. He used the back of a wooden shovel as a slate and a piece of charcoal as a pencil.

A kindly woman stood over him, encouraging him to keep trying. The woman was his stepmother. The boy grew into manhood without showing signs of greatness. He studied law, but his success in that profession was meager.

He tried store keeping; he entered the army, but made no noteworthy record at either. Everything to which he turned his hand seemed to wither into failure. Then it is said a great love came into his life. It ended with the death of the one he loved. But the sorrow over that death reached deeply into the man's soul and there it made contact with the secret power that comes only from within.

PUT POWER TO WORK

He seized that power and put it to work. It made him President of the United States. It wiped out slavery in America. And it saved the Union from dissolution.

So, this power that comes to men from within knows no social caste, no insurmountable obstacles, no unsolvable problems. It is available to the poor and the humble as it is to the rich and the powerful. It is possessed by all who think accurately. It cannot be put into effect for you by anyone except yourself.

What strange fear invades the minds of men and short-circuits their approach to that secret power which can lift them to great heights of achievement?

How and why do the vast majority of people become the victims of a negative hypnotic rhythm which destroys their capacity to use the secret power of their own minds?

The approach to all genius has been charted. It is the self-same path followed by all great leaders who have contributed to our American way of life.

HOW TO TAP POWER

"How may one tap that secret power that comes from within?" you ask. Let us see how others have drawn upon it.

A young clergyman by the name of Frank Gunsaulus had long desired to build a new type of college. He knew exactly what he wanted, but the hitch was that it required a million dollars in cash.

He made up his mind to get the million dollars! Definiteness of decision, based on definiteness of purpose, constituted the first step of his plan. Then he wrote a sermon entitled "What I Would Do With a Million Dollars." He announced in the Chicago newspapers that he would preach on that subject the next Sunday morning.

At the end of the sermon a strange man, whom the preacher had never seen before, walked down to the pulpit, and said, "I liked your sermon. You may come down to my office and I will give you the million dollars you need."

The stranger was Philip Armour, founder of Armour & Co., meat packers.

APPLIED FAITH

This is the sum and the substance of what happened, and the power which made it happen was applied faith—faith backed by actions—not mere passive faith.

Faith, rightly understood, is always active—not passive. Passive faith has no more power than an idle dynamo. To generate power, the machine must be set into motion. Active faith knows no fear, no self-imposed limitations. Reinforced with faith, the weakest mortal is mightier than disaster, stronger than failure, more powerful than fear.

The emergencies of life often bring men to crossroads where they are forced to choose between roads marked Faith and Fear. What is it that causes the vast majority to take the Fear road? The choice hinges upon one's mental attitude, and the Creator has so arranged man's powers that each individual controls his own.

THE FAITH ROAD

The man who takes the Faith road is the man who has conditioned his mind to believe. He has conditioned it a little at a time by prompt and courageous decisions and actions in the details of his daily work. The man who takes the Fear road does so because he has neglected to condition his mind to a positive attitude.

Search until you find the point of approach to that secret power from within. When you find it you will have discovered your true self—that "other self" who makes use of every experience of life. Then, whether you build a better mousetrap, write a better book, or preach a better sermon, the world will make a beaten path to your door, recognize you and adequately reward you. Success will be yours no matter who you are or what may have been the nature and scope of your past failures.

Article IX

DEVELOP A
PLEASING PERSONALITY:
PLEASING MIND IS BEST ASSET

Your personality is the sample case which shows what you have to offer. Fortunately, a pleasing personality can be developed by anyone with enough self-discipline to discover his faults and correct them. When the job is done properly a pleasing personality can become one's greatest asset—because with it he can sell his way through life on his own terms.

Franklin D. Roosevelt groomed his personality with such painstaking care that it made him one of our most popular presidents. It served him so well that he sold himself into the presidency for four terms.

President Eisenhower, with his sincere personal warmth, is another example of the heights to which an individual can rise through a pleasing personality.

Your personality consists of the sum total of all those mental and physical traits which distinguish you from all others, for better or for worse. It is the most important factor in determining whether you are liked or disliked. It is the medium by which you negotiate your way through life. And it determines your ability to negotiate with others to get their friendly cooperation.

BONUS FOR PERSONALITY

Charles M. Schwab's pleasing personality lifted him from day laborer to a high executive position at a salary of $75,000 a year, and he often received a bonus of $1,000,000. His employer, Andrew Carnegie, said the yearly salary was for the work Schwab performed, but the bonus was for what Schwab, with his pleasing personality, could get others to do.

If you want a "million-dollar personality" you can have it if you:

1. Develop a positive mental attitude and let it be seen and felt by others.
2. Train your voice to be pleasing by always speaking in a carefully disciplined friendly tone.
3. Keep your mind alert and be willing to listen when others are conversing with you. "Getting someone else told" may feed the ego but it never attracts people or makes friends.
4. Be flexible in all of your relations with others. Adjust yourself to all circumstances, pleasant or otherwise, without losing your composure or showing your temper. Remember that silence may be much more effective than your angry words.

DEVELOP PATIENCE

5. Develop patience. Remember that proper timing of your words and acts may give you a big advantage over impatient people. If you are a salesman, perhaps you should read the foregoing sentence two or three times.

6. Keep an open mind on all subjects and toward all people. Favorable opportunities never break down the doors to closed minds. Intolerance does not lead to wisdom.

7. Learn to smile when you are speaking to others so that they know you are a friendly person. Franklin D. Roosevelt's "million-dollar smile" was his greatest asset.

8. Be tactful in your speech and manners. Keep in mind that not all thoughts you may have should be expressed, even if they are true.

9. Be prompt in your decisions after you have all of the necessary facts on which to base them. Remember that procrastination reveals to others a negative trait of character which is somehow associated with fear.

GOOD DEED A DAY

10. Engage in at least one good deed each day in which you will praise or serve one or more people without expecting reward. Watch how rapidly your list of friends will grow!

11. When you meet defeat, instead of brooding over it search carefully for that "seed of an equivalent benefit" it is sure to contain. Express your gratitude for having gained a measure of wisdom which would not come without defeat.

12. And remember, always, that the person to whom you are speaking, at any given time, is the most important person in the world. You may have his good will by asking him questions and giving *him* a chance to talk.

13. Praise the good traits of others, but don't rub it on where it is not deserved or spread it too thickly.

14. Lastly, have someone whom you trust, who has the courage to be honest with you, point out to you traits of personality you could do without.

Article X

USE YOUR PERSONAL INITIATIVE: HOW TO DEVELOP YOUR INITIATIVE

D o the thing and you shall have the power," said Emerson. It would be difficult to name a more destructive human habit than that of procrastination—putting off until tomorrow that which should have been done last week. Personal initiative is the only cure for procrastination.

Successful people in all walks of life are individuals who think and move on their own personal initiative. There are two forms of action: (1) that in which one engages from choice and (2) that in which one indulges only by force of necessity.

We live in a country noted throughout the world as a nation which abounds in the privilege of personal freedom available to rich and poor alike. It is perhaps the most important factor in our system of free enterprise.

The privilege of personal initiative was considered of

such great importance that it is specifically guaranteed to every citizen in the Constitution of the United States. And it is of such great importance that every well-managed business recognizes and properly rewards individuals who use their initiative to better the business.

RESIGNATION REFUSED

When Andrew Carnegie was a young clerk in the office of the Division Superintendent of the Pennsylvania Railroad Co., in Pittsburgh, he came to the office one morning before his boss arrived and discovered there had been a bad railroad wreck just outside of the city. He tried furiously to reach his boss by telephone.

Finally, in desperation, he did something which he knew could mean his automatic discharge because of the company's strict rules. Recognizing that every minute of delay was costing the railroad company a fortune, he wired the conductor of the wrecked train giving him orders what to do. He signed his boss' name to the message.

When his boss came to his desk several hours later he found Carnegie's resignation and an explanation of what he had done. The day passed by and nothing happened. The next day Carnegie's resignation was sent back to him with these words written across the face in red ink: *"RESIGNA-TION REFUSED!"*

Several days later his boss called Carnegie into his office and said, "Young man, there are two kinds of people who never get ahead or amount to anything. One is the fellow who will not do what he is told, and the other is the fellow who will not do anything more than he is told."

MADE IDEA PAY

There was a sermon on personal initiative in one brief sentence. You may wish to copy it and paste it on the mirror where you can see it daily.

A few years ago, George Stefek, of Chicago, was convalescing at Hines Veterans Hospital. As he lay there, he got an idea. The idea was simple. Anyone else could have had it! But the important thing is that Stefek acted on it as soon as he got out of the hospital. Today it is paying off handsomely.

He noticed that shirts returned from laundries were stiffened with a blank piece of cardboard. He discovered that these cardboards cost the laundries $3.00 per thousand. Stefek's idea was to sell advertising space on the cardboards. As a result he could sell them to the laundries for $1.00 per thousand. Now laundries are saving money—advertisers have a new medium to reach prospects—and George Stefek's American Shirtboard Advertising Co. is a thriving business.

Clarence Saunders of Memphis, Tenn., saw a long line of people waiting to serve themselves in a then new type of restaurant—a cafeteria. He put his imagination to work and came up with a plan for "borrowing" the self-help plan for his employer, a local grocer.

STARTED SUPER-MARKET

When he told the grocer his idea he was informed that he was being paid to pack and deliver groceries—not to waste his time with foolish, impractical ideas. Clarence quit his job and carried out his self-help grocery plan under the name of Piggly Wiggly stores. He made it pay off to the tune of four million dollars the first four years. Moreover, his plan was taken over by other grocers and it is now the method of merchandising used in our great super-markets.

Doubtlessly, by giving man absolute control over his power to think, the Creator intended that man should use that prerogative through his own initiative.

That overworked alibi of the procrastinator—"I haven't had time"—probably has caused more failures than all other alibis combined. The man who gets ahead and makes a place for himself *always finds time* to move on his own initiative in any direction necessary for his advancement or benefit.

Article XI

BE ENTHUSIASTIC:
ENTHUSIASM KEY TO
MANY DOORS

N othing great was ever accomplished without enthusiasm," said Emerson. In the great Mormon Tabernacle in Salt Lake City a guest speaker was billed to speak for forty-five minutes. He spoke for more than two hours. When he finished ten thousand men and women arose and cheered him for five minutes.

What did the speaker say? That was not as important as the way he said it! The crowd was swept away by the speaker's enthusiasm. It is doubtful whether a single person remembered what he said.

Louis Victor Eytinge was serving a life sentence in the Arizona State prison. He had no friends. He had no lawyer—no money. But he did have enthusiasm which he used so effectively that it brought him freedom.

Eytinge wrote a letter to the Remington Typewriter Company telling of his plight and requesting that the company sell him a typewriter on credit. The company did better than that. It gave him a typewriter.

EARNS PARDON

He began writing business firms asking for their sales literature which he rewrote and returned to them. His copy writing was so effective that he soon had enough money, from voluntary donations, to hire a lawyer.

His work came to the attention of a big New York City advertising agency which, in conjunction with the lawyer, got him pardoned. As he walked out of prison he was met by the agency head who greeted him with these words: "Well, Eytinge, your enthusiasm has proved more powerful than the iron bars of this prison."

The advertising agency had a job waiting for him at a salary of $10,000 a year.

MIAMI STORY TOLD

During the recent housing shortage, W. Clement Stone of Chicago, president of the Combined Insurance Company of America, took his family to Miami for a vacation. When he applied to a real estate broker to rent a house the broker laughed.

"Why," exclaimed the broker, "you couldn't rent a house in this city for love or money."

Stone smiled and said, "You just watch me and see!"

Meanwhile his family was waiting in a hotel lobby. He called a taxicab and began a systematic drive through the city. In a little while he saw a large estate, enclosed by a huge iron fence, with a "for sale" sign on it. He got the name of the owner from the caretaker, telephoned him in another city, and persuaded him to rent the house at a very modest sum, on the theory that an occupied house would sell more rapidly than a vacant house.

Two things did it! A sound sales talk and *enthusiasm!* Logic, alone, wouldn't have done the trick.

BILLY GRAHAM CITED

Oral Roberts and Billy Graham, preaching to unprecedented audiences all over the world, are gaining converts to Christianity in unbelievable numbers: Take enthusiasm out of their ministry and they would lose all their effectiveness.

Clarence Darrow was perhaps the greatest lawyer this nation has ever produced. His success was due, in a large measure, to his great capacity for expressing himself with enthusiasm and his ability to arouse enthusiasm in his listeners, courts and juries alike. As far as knowledge of the law was concerned, Darrow was no better than the majority of lawyers of his time.

Someone has said—and I wish I had been the one—"There is rejoicing in Heaven and the gritting of teeth in Hell when the great God turns loose a man on earth with a capacity for unlimited use of *faith* and *enthusiasm*."

How does one become enthusiastic? By acting enthusiastically in thoughts, words and deeds. A life insurance salesman, who is perhaps the greatest salesman in his field, sends himself a telegram every night so it will be on the breakfast table the next morning. It tells him how much insurance he is going to sell that day. And he does it. Sometimes he goes far beyond the mark he has set.

The telegrams are signed: *DOCTOR ENTHUSIASM.*

If you think the plan is fantastic, or even foolish, just remember that this man leads all other salesmen in one of the largest life insurance companies in America.

Article XII

CONTROL YOUR
ATTENTION:
ONE-TRACK MIND
SIGN OF LEADER

Perhaps the one human trait which stands out above all others as an aid to success is the fixed habit of turning on more will power instead of quitting when the going becomes hard and defeat seems imminent.

Development of this habit begins with the adoption of a definite purpose fanned into a white heat of enthusiasm through accurate thinking, applied faith and self-discipline.

Henry Ford's success was largely due to the fact that he concentrated all of his resources—spiritual, mental, physical and financial—behind his definite major purpose, the manufacturing of a low-priced dependable automobile.

His dogged determination was illustrated when he gave

the order to his engineers to cast an automobile engine block in one piece instead of two, as had been the practice.

"Impossible," said the engineers.

"You use that word too loosely!" Ford exploded. "Go ahead and try."

A month passed and no engine cylinder block appeared. Ford called all of his engineers in and said, "Gentlemen, if I don't have a satisfactory cylinder block cast in one piece within one week there'll be a new staff of engineers here to take your place."

The cylinder block came through in a hurry.

Comic Danny Thomas tried for years to find a way to stay in his beloved show business and yet come home to his family each night. By concentrating his mind on that purpose in a spirit of intense applied faith he found the answer to his desire through television.

The most successful people in all callings are those with a so-called one-track mind: that is, a mind that is controlled and concentrated upon one thing at a time.

When Martin W. Littleton was a young lad, he came into the general store of his small Texas home town, where a number of the local townspeople were warming themselves by the stove.

"Martin," one of them jeeringly asked, "what are you going to be when you grow up?" Looking the jester squarely in the eye Martin replied, "I'm going to be the best lawyer in the United States."

By concentrating on the study of law Martin Littleton

made good his assertion. He became the highest paid lawyer in America, retained by many large corporations, such as Standard Oil.

F. W. Woolworth concentrated on Five and Ten Cent Stores and made himself fabulously rich. Marconi concentrated upon the study of wireless communication and lived to see his efforts lay the foundation for radio, television and radar.

Noah Webster concentrated on and gave us the modern English dictionary.

RANGE LIMITLESS

The range of purposes on which man can successfully direct his mind, through concentration, is limitless. Every living creature below man concentrates its efforts on but two ends, reproduction and food.

Other physical manifestations of the law of concentration are seen in the sun that sets and rises with uninterrupted regularity—water that flows downhill in response to the law of gravitation—the seasons of the year which inevitably come—and every living thing, including man, reproducing itself after its kind.

Here is evidence that the law of concentration is not man-made, because none of man's efforts has ever interrupted any of these manifestations of the Creator's purpose.

Determine what you want most from life. Adopt that as your definite major purpose. Make the start toward your goal right where you stand. When you come to those uphill pulls where the going is hard, back it with all the enthusiasm at your command, and lo! You will find yourself in the right path.

You will be on the "success beam" that will carry you unerringly to the object of your aims and purposes. Try it! It works.

Article XIII

WORK WITH YOUR TEAM: GOLDEN RULE KEY TO COOPERATION

There are two kinds of cooperation. One is based on the motive of fear or need. The other is based upon voluntary willingness. Cooperation is indispensable in your home, in your job, in your social life. It is an absolute necessity in our form of government and system of free enterprise.

Teamwork can be acquired only by establishing the proper motive to induce friendly coordination of effort.

Andrew Carnegie's method of inspiring teamwork has never been improved upon.

First, he established a monetary motive through promotions and bonuses to suit each individual's job, designed so that a part of the individual's income depended on the sort of service he rendered.

Second, he never reprimanded any employee openly. But he caused the employee to reprimand himself, by asking carefully directed questions.

Third, he never made decisions for his executives. He encouraged them to make their own and to be responsible for the results.

UPPER LEVEL SUCCESS

Success on the upper levels of achievement is attained only by teamwork. This means *giving* cooperation as well as *receiving* it. Selfish leaders will get little cooperation from their subordinates because cooperation is something like love in that one must give it in order to get it.

Those of you who have flown on any Capital Airlines planes must have observed the friendly spirit of the crew which is picked up by passengers. That friendliness is not accidental. It emanates from the president of the Capital Airlines and his assistant and goes right down the line of authority to the humblest position.

The same friendly cooperation is apparent on Capt. Eddie Rickenbacker's Eastern Air Lines. Rickenbacker is noted as a leader who inspires teamwork. During World War I, in which he personally knocked down 26 German planes, his leadership inspired the famed "Hat-in-the-Ring" squadron to heights of glory. And in World War II, it was his personal example that forged a group of airmen into a team and brought them through safely when they were cast adrift on an open raft in the Pacific for almost a month.

CAN INFLUENCE OTHERS

William James, a Harvard University professor, once said, "If you can influence others to cooperate with you in a friendly spirit, you can get anything you want with but little or no resistance." Quite a broad statement, but it happens to be true.

Get at the heart of successful corporations like the Bell Telephone Co. or any of the electric power companies, and you will find that teamwork, inspired from the top downward, is what makes them "tick."

Whenever you find a sports team that is out front, you will observe that the credit goes not to any one person, unless it is the coach who inspires his players to subordinate personal glory to the success of the team. Knute Rockne of Notre Dame was a wonderful example of a leader who could inspire teamwork.

It is difficult to give an adequate interpretation of the motives which induce friendly teamwork without calling attention to the Sermon on the Mount. No better way of getting friendly cooperation than by the application of the Golden Rule has ever been discovered.

There is a law of reciprocation which has a negative—the law of retaliation. They both are deeply seated in the nature of man. Through them the meaning of that Biblical passage, "Whatsoever a man soweth that shall he also reap," becomes crystal clear. For it is true that whatever you do to or for another you do to or for yourself.

Work well with your team—and your team will carry you to success.

Article XIV

LEARN FROM DEFEAT:
REVERSE OFTEN
MEANS VICTORY

Every adversity, every failure and every unpleasant experience carries with it the seed of an equivalent benefit which may prove a blessing in disguise.

Failure and defeat are the common language in which Nature speaks to all men and brings them under a spirit of humility so that they may acquire wisdom and understanding.

A wise man once said that it would be impossible to live with a person who had never failed or been defeated in any of his purposes. This same man also discovered that people achieve successes in almost exact proportion to the extent to which they meet and master adversity and defeat.

And he made another important discovery—that the truly great achievements were attained by men and women past the age of 50 years, and he expressed the opinion that the most productive years of men engaged in brain work were from 60–70.

Abraham Lincoln lost his mother when he was a very young child. "No seed of an equivalent benefit in that," some may say. But his loss brought him a stepmother whose influence fired him with ambition to educate himself and rise in life.

MARSHALL FIELD'S VOW

Marshall Field lost his retail store in the great Chicago fire and with it almost all his money. Pointing to the smoldering ashes he said, "On this very spot I will build the greatest retail store in the world." The great Marshall Field & Co. store which now stands at State and Randolph Streets in Chicago, testifies that there is the seed of an equivalent benefit in every adversity. Sometimes it takes courage, faith and imagination to reveal that seed and germinate it into the full-blown flower of benefit. But it is always there.

Consider, for example, the case of Michael L. Benedum who is, at 86, the world's greatest oil wildcatter—with a personal fortune of more than $100,000,000.

Ask him the secret of his success, and Mike Benedum will tell you: "I learned to keep right on going when things got tough." For example, he had barely made his first fortune when he took some bad advice—and lost his shirt.

Benedum turned defeat into victory by learning a prime lesson: to rely on his own judgment for crucial decisions. Consequently, he "kept right on going" to discover more oil reserves throughout the world than the total of petroleum that has been used by mankind in all of history.

PHYSICAL HANDICAPS

In 1920, adversity hit him again when he failed in an attempt to find productive oil reserves in the Philippines. Benedum bounced back, saying, "It's part of the game. You can't find oil everywhere. If you did, there'd be no fun in wildcatting."

Our American society is replete with examples of people who achieved fame and fortune by overcoming adversity. Even physical ailments and handicaps need not impede you—as evidenced by Franklin D. Roosevelt, Theodore Roosevelt, Helen Keller and Thomas Edison.

Learn from defeat as did Richard M. Davis of Morgantown, West Virginia, who fought his way up in the coal mining business—only to lose everything, including his home and furniture, in the Depression. He learned that his reputation, which he thus salvaged by refusing to go into bankruptcy, was his great asset. With this alone, he overcame the challenge of adversity and paid off his indebtedness of almost $150,000.

Today, Davis is the president of the Davis-Wilson Coal Co. at Morgantown and in addition to possessing great wealth, is one of the recognized leaders in the fight for international peace.

FACTS OF LIFE

You too can ride the success beam by learning to discover and build on the seed of an equivalent benefit in each of your setbacks.

Two important facts of life stand out boldly! One is that defeat in some form inevitably overtakes each of us, at one time or another. The other is that every adversity brings the seed of an equivalent benefit, often in some hidden form.

From analysis of these two facts it is not difficult to recognize that the Creator intends man to gain strength, understanding and wisdom through struggle. Adversity and defeat cause man to develop his wits and go forward.

It is often difficult for us to recognize the potentiality of an equivalent benefit in our adversities while we are still suffering from the wounds. But Time, the greatest of all healers, will disclose them to those who sincerely search for and believe that they will find them.

Article XV

CULTIVATE CREATIVE VISION:
CREATIVE VISION IS
SIXTH SENSE

You have at your command the power of imagination in two forms. One is known as synthetic imagination. This consists of some combination of known ideas, concepts, plans or facts, arranged in a *new* combination.

The other is known as creative imagination. It operates through the sixth sense and serves as the medium by which basically new facts or ideas are revealed. It is also the medium for inspiration.

Thomas A. Edison used synthetic imagination to invent the incandescent electric lamp by bringing together in a new way, two well-known principles. Long before Edison's time it was known that light could be produced with electricity by applying that energy to a wire and setting up a short circuit. But no one had found a way to keep the metal from burning out quickly.

EDISON'S DISCOVERY

Edison discovered how to do this by the application of the principle by which charcoal is produced, namely, wood is set on fire, then covered with dirt so that only enough oxygen can get to the fire to keep it smoldering but not blazing.

Taking his cue from the principle that nothing can burn without oxygen, Edison placed a wire in a bottle, pumped out all the air. Then he applied electricity to the projecting wires and lo! The first incandescent electric lamp was born.

Dr. Elmer R. Gates, of Chevy Chase, Maryland, gives us a good example of creative imagination. He had to his credit more patents than Edison. Most of them were perfected by the application of his sixth sense, which he developed to a high degree.

By shutting himself in a soundproof room and turning off the lights, Dr. Gates managed to eliminate all physical interferences so that he could concentrate on attaining information he desired. When the information came through, by way of his sixth sense, he switched on the lights and immediately wrote it down. Strangely, sometimes ideas were revealed for which he had not been searching, a fact which was largely responsible for the great number of inventions he perfected.

SIXTH SENSE

Your five physical senses give you contact with the physical world and make available to you its nature and usages. But your sixth sense which operates through the subconscious section of your mind, gives you contact with the invisible forces of the universe. It makes available to you knowledge you could not acquire through your limited physical senses.

R. G. LeTourneau, the world-renowned industrialist, performs near miracles in the production of machines which the most astute engineers say are virtually impossible, even though he has had little or no technical training in mechanics. He uses a system similar to that employed by Edison and produces mechanical devices which do almost everything but talk.

George Parker, founder of the famous Parker Pen Co., directed his entire business affairs to an enviable plane of achievement by making use of his sixth sense. And it has been said that George Eastman, famous camera manufacturer, attained success the same way.

The sixth sense of creative vision becomes more dependable through systematic regular use, as do the five physical senses.

FONTAINEBLEAU VISION

All people on the upper levels of success have some system for conditioning their minds to get and remain on the "success beam." Some successful people make use of a mind conditioning system *without recognizing what they are doing.*

It was creative vision which led to the establishment of the luxurious Fontainebleau Hotel at Miami Beach.

Hotelman Ben Novack arrived at Miami in 1940 with just $1,800—and a dream! His dream was for a beautiful resort hostelry which would be known throughout the world for the comfort and the relaxation it offered.

By judicious pyramiding of his meager resources and the enthusiasm with which he conveyed his dream to financiers, Novack put his creative vision to work and December a year ago saw the Fontainebleau open its door to the first guest.

Clarence Birdseye, as a fur trapper in Labrador, once sampled some cabbage that had accidentally frozen. From the experience, he came up with the idea of merchandising quick-frozen foods.

PUT DREAMS TO WORK

Are *you* making *your* dreams work for you, through creative vision, as Ben Novack and Clarence Birdseye did?

A very effective method of making use of the sixth sense is to write out a clear, concise description of the problem you wish solved, or the objective you desire to attain. Repeat this several times a day in the form of a prayer. The prayer should be founded on unshakable faith so definite and strong that you can see yourself already in possession of your objective.

If at first trial this method does not bring the desired

results, keep on trying. Each time express gratitude as if you had already attained your objective, even though it has not yet come into your physical possession.

The master-key to success lies in your capacity to believe that you will succeed. Remember, whatever your mind can conceive and believe, your mind can achieve.

BUDGET YOUR TIME AND
MONEY: CONSERVE HOURS
TO WIN DOLLARS

John Wanamaker, the Philadelphia merchant king, once said, "The man who doesn't have a fixed system for the proper use of his time and money will never have financial security unless he has a rich relative who will leave him a fortune."

Your time is one of your greatest assets! It is the one asset you can change into any form of riches you choose. Or you spend your entire lifetime without plan or purpose beyond that of procuring food and shelter.

If you want to live a well-balanced, successful life, you should recognize the need for a systematic schedule by which to direct your time to ends that will insure success.

The average person's time can be divided into three parts—one for sleep, one for work and one for recreation.

FREE TIME MOST VITAL

Sound health demands at least eight hours' sleep a day for the average person. From eight to ten hours a day are required for work. This leaves from six to eight hours a day of free time which one may use as he pleases.

This is the most important part of the day, as far as your personal achievement is concerned. It provides you with the opportunity for self-improvement and education by which your working hours can be marketed for a higher price. The person who uses his free time solely for personal pleasure and play will never be a success at anything.

Your sleep period is necessary for your health. Therefore don't cut into it. Your work period requires all your thoughts and actions for specific duties. Therefore the only opportunity it offers for self-improvement is through modification of the quality and the quantity of service you render.

Your free time period is just what it implies—time that you may use as you please. During this time one may not only plant the seed of future opportunities, but he may also cause that seed to germinate and grow into some form of self-advancement.

HENRY CROWN AN EXAMPLE

Henry Crown, Chicago industrialist, through judicious budgeting of his time manages to execute a wide variety of activities. Not only does he head the vast Material Service

Corporation, but he also heads a syndicate which owns the Empire State Building.

Free time can also be effectively used in association with carefully selected companions who can inspire and aid you in gaining success.

"Show me a man's closest associates," said Thomas A. Edison, "and I will tell you what sort of character the man has and where he is going in life."

Your free time is strictly your own. If you value it properly you can use it to build friendships that will be an asset to you when you need help. You should divide it into several parts—some of it to self-improvement, some to recreation and relaxation, some to a hobby.

One's free time may be properly called "opportunity time." For many it proves only to be one's "misfortune time." For it is during this period that most people acquire their negative habits, which vitally affect their work time. Such habits include, for example, stealing their sleep time for purposes which yield them no benefits.

BUDGETING ESSENTIAL

How should one budget his income and outgo of money?

The successful man budgets his money as carefully as he budgets his time. He sets aside a definite amount for food, clothing and household expenses, for insurance, for savings and investments, for charity and for recreation. The amount devoted to each depends, of course, upon one's occupation and earning ability.

A single man should save a much larger percentage of his income than it is possible for a married man to save, since generally he has fewer dependents. But every person, man or woman, should save a definite percentage, even if it is not more than five percent.

In times of emergency even a modest bank account can give you courage and security. In times of prosperity it will bolster your self-confidence and save you anxiety. Worry over money matters can kill your ambition . . . and you!

Article XVII

KEEP HEALTHY:
KEEP A POSITIVE
MENTAL ATTITUDE

Your brain is the unchallengeable boss of your body. One of the most important requirements in developing good health is to maintain a positive mental attitude.

A negative mental attitude serves as a perfect foundation for hypochondria—imaginary ailments. A large percentage of the work doctors perform today is in the field of "psychosomatics."

Sound health begins with sound health consciousness— just as financial prosperity begins with prosperity consciousness.

How can you develop a sound health consciousness? Think in terms of sound health. Talk in terms of sound health. Exercise temperance in all things, especially in eating and in the use of intoxicants.

Your mental attitude affects every function of your body.

Food in excess or in the wrong combination can be as

deadly as poison. Of course you know that fear, anxiety, anger, jealousy, worry and hatred indulged in while eating can be exceedingly harmful.

LIQUOR POISONOUS

Too much liquor or other intoxicants mixed with food destroys a portion of the value of the food and sets up a condition of poison. What is "too much" depends somewhat on who is taking it and his general health condition.

The old saying, "Some people dig their graves with their teeth," is no mere wise-crack. It is true. Your body needs every essential vitamin and mineral. Sometimes it is essential to add food supplements and vitamins to your diet in order to give your body necessary vitality and vigor to carry you to success.

Healthful food must be grown from soil which is known to contain all of the mineral elements that are required in foods to give them the values essential for the maintenance of sound health.

Sound health calls for a balanced way of living so that the "invisible doctor" who works within the body night and day may have time to correct the damage the individual does to his body by neglect or lack of knowledge of the rules of sound health.

Psychiatrists and psychologists have discovered that sound health depends to an astounding degree on the balance of love and worship, work and play.

WORK AND PLAY

Any well-informed layman knows that work must be balanced with relaxation and play to maintain sound health. But not until recent years has it been known except by experts that love and worship must also be controlled and balanced for the sake of sound health.

Here are some general rules to help you maintain sound health: Have a competent doctor, in whom you have full confidence, give you a thorough checkup at least once a year. If any hidden causes of ill health are present, the doctor will most likely find them and eliminate them. His pronouncement that you are "as sound as a dollar" will give confidence worth far more than his charges.

If you are not getting all necessary vitamins and minerals from your regular diet, have a competent food specialist or dietician recommend the type and quantity of food supplement you need.

Stick strictly to his recommendations. Don't try to be "your own doctor" in the matter of food supplements.

Get your mental attitude under control and keep it there. Follow the sixteen rules which have been presented in this column, starting with Definiteness of Purpose, Applied Faith, Enthusiasm, and the habit of Going the Extra Mile.

A healthy body will help you attain peace of mind and financial prosperity.

Article XVIII

LET HABITS WORK FOR
YOU: HABIT IS LADDER
TO RICHER LIFE

A ll of your successes and your failures are the results of the habits you have formed. There are two types of habits—those which we form deliberately and voluntarily for definite purposes, and those which we permit to be formed by the chance circumstances of life through lack of an organized philosophy or work-plan by which to provide an ordered life.

Both of these types of habits operate automatically, once they have been accepted by the individual; both are directly controlled by the great universal law which I call "Cosmic Habit-Force."

It seems quite evident to me that Cosmic Habit-Force is the overall comptroller through which Nature directs all of her laws. Through it she maintains the existing relationship between the atoms of matter, the stars and planets in the heavens, the seasons of the year, sickness and health, life and death. It could be the medium through which thought is translated into its physical equivalent.

You, of course, know that Nature maintains a perfect balance between all of the elements of matter and energy throughout the universe; that the maintenance is systematic, automatic and orderly. You can see the stars and planets move with perfect timing and precision, each keeping its own place in time and space.

You can see that an oak tree grows from an acorn, always, and a pine tree grows from the seed of its ancestor. And you know that Nature never makes a mistake and grows a pine tree from an acorn, nor an oak tree from the seed of a pine.

There are facts you can see. But do you recognize that they do not "just happen" by chance—something has to make them happen! That something is the power which fixes habits and makes them permanent. Man is the only creature which the Creator permits the privilege of fixing his own habits to suit his own desires.

We are ruled by habits, all of us! Our habits are fastened upon us by repetition of our thoughts and acts. Therefore we can control our earthly destinies and our way of living only to the extent that we control our thoughts. We must direct them to form the sort of habits we need to serve as our road map to guide our lives. Good habits which lead to success can be ordered and used by any individual. Bad habits can be broken and replaced by good ones at will by anyone.

MAN HAS CONTROL

The habits of every living creature except man are fixed by what we call "instinct." This places them under limitations from which they cannot escape.

The Creator not only gave men complete, unchallengeable control over the power of thought, but with this gift came the means of possessing thought power and directing it to any desired end.

The Creator has also given man another privilege whereby thoughts are made to clothe themselves in their physical likeness and equivalent.

Here, then, is a profound truth. With it you may open doors to wisdom and live an ordered life, you will be able to control those factors necessary to your success.

The rewards available to the person who takes possession of his own mind power and directs it to definite ends of his own choice are great in number. But penalties for not doing so are equally great in number.

NO MIRACLES WROUGHT

Cosmic Habit-Force works no miracles, makes no attempt to create something out of nothing, nor does it suggest what course anyone should follow. But it does help an individual—nay, it forces him—to proceed naturally and logically to convert his thoughts into their physical equivalent by using the natural media that is available to him which are related to his thinking.

When you begin reorganizing your habits and building new ones, start with the success habit. Put yourself on the "success beam" by concentrating your daily thoughts on whatever you desire. In due time these new thought-habits will lead you unerringly to fame and fortune.

"Whatever the mind can conceive and believe, the mind can achieve."

Napoleon Hill

FOR MORE INFORMATION ABOUT NAPOLEON
HILL AND AVAILABLE PRODUCTS, PLEASE
CONTACT THE FOLLOWING LOCATIONS:

Napoleon Hill World Learning Center
Purdue University Calumet
2300 173rd Street
Hammond, Indiana 46323-2094

Judith Williamson, Director
Uriel "Chino" Martinez, Assistant and Graphic Designer
Telephone: 219.989.3173 or 219.989.3166
Email: nhf@purduecal.edu

The Napoleon Hill Foundation University of Virginia—Wise College
Relations
1 College Avenue
Wise, Virginia 24293

Don Green, Executive Director
Annedia Sturgill, Executive Assistant
Telephone: 276.328.6700
Email: napoleonhill@uvawise.edu
Website: www.naphill.org

If you enjoyed this book, visit

www.tarcherbooks.com

and sign up for Tarcher's e-newsletter to receive
special offers, giveaway promotions, and
information on hot upcoming releases.

Great Lives Begin with Great Ideas

Connect with the Tarcher Community

· · ·

Stay in touch with favorite authors!
Enter weekly contests!
Read exclusive excerpts!
Voice your opinions!

Follow us

 Tarcher Books

@TarcherBooks

If you would like to place a bulk order
of this book, call 1-800-847-5515.

PLEA
ADVANTAGE
OF THE
CHAMBERMAID

PLEASE TAKE ADVANTAGE OF THE CHAMBERMAID

and other silly signs

**Compiled by
John Jerome**

MICHAEL O'MARA BOOKS LIMITED

First published in Great Britain in 1997 by
Michael O'Mara Books Limited
9 Lion Yard
Tremadoc Road
London SW4 7NQ

Copyright in this compilation
© Michael O'Mara Books Limited 1997

A CIP catalogue record for this book is available
from the British Library

ISBN 1-85479-316-0

3 5 7 9 10 8 6 4 2

Designed by Mick Keates
Typset by Concise Artisans
Printed and bound by Cox & Wyman, Reading

BECAUSE OF THE
IMPROPRIETY OF
ENTERTAINING
GUESTS OF THE
OPPOSITE SEX IN
THE BEDROOM, IT
IS SUGGESTED
THAT THE LOBBY
BE USED FOR THIS
PURPOSE

ZURICH HOTEL

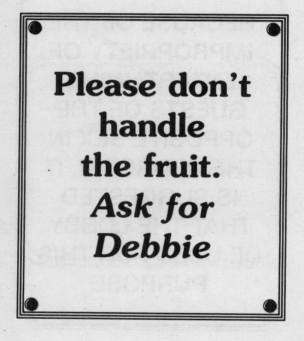

Please don't handle the fruit. *Ask for Debbie*

GREENGROCER'S

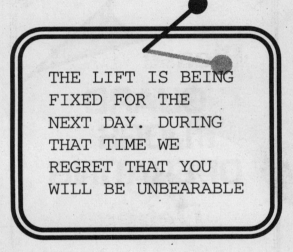

THE LIFT IS BEING
FIXED FOR THE
NEXT DAY. DURING
THAT TIME WE
REGRET THAT YOU
WILL BE UNBEARABLE

BUCHAREST HOTEL LOBBY

GUARD
DOGS
OPERATING

DISTRICT HOSPITAL

Our
wines
leave you
nothing to
hope for

SWISS RESTAURANT

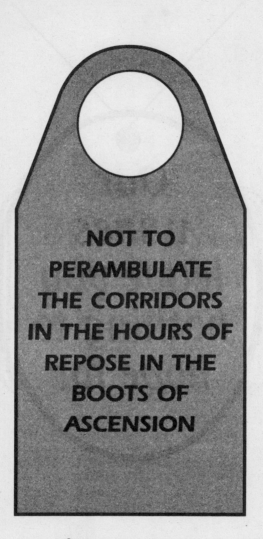

NOT TO
PERAMBULATE
THE CORRIDORS
IN THE HOURS OF
REPOSE IN THE
BOOTS OF
ASCENSION

AUSTRIAN SKI HOTEL

WE STAND BEHIND EVERY BED WE SELL

FURNITURE SHOP

YOU ARE WELCOME TO
VISIT THE CEMETERY
WHERE FAMOUS
RUSSIAN AND SOVIET
COMPOSERS, ARTISTS
AND WRITERS ARE
BURIED DAILY...
EXCEPT THURSDAY

MOSCOW HOTEL
(across the street from a
Russian Orthodox Monastery)

**ST JUST
CHURCH
AND BAR**

CORNISH ROAD SIGN

YOU ARE
INVITED TO
TAKE
ADVANTAGE
OF THE
CHAMBERMAID

JAPANESE HOTEL

WARNING: NEVER USE WHILE SLEEPING

WARNING WITH HAIR DRYER

IF YOU WISH
BREAKFAST, LIFT THE
TELEPHONE AND OUR
WAITRESS WILL ARRIVE.
THIS WILL BE ENOUGH
TO BRING UP YOUR
FOOD

TEL AVIV HOTEL

DON'T GO INTO ANOTHER SHOP TO BE CHEATED – COME IN HERE

BARGAIN BASEMENT

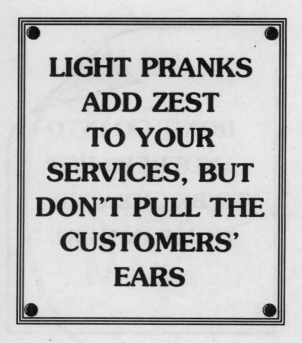

**LIGHT PRANKS
ADD ZEST
TO YOUR
SERVICES, BUT
DON'T PULL THE
CUSTOMERS'
EARS**

SPECIAL
TODAY...
NO ICE
CREAM

SWISS MOUNTAIN INN

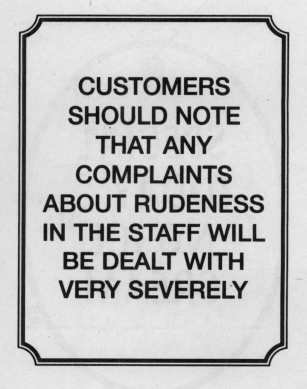

CUSTOMERS
SHOULD NOTE
THAT ANY
COMPLAINTS
ABOUT RUDENESS
IN THE STAFF WILL
BE DEALT WITH
VERY SEVERELY

BRITISH HOTEL

AFTER ONE VISIT WE GUARANTEE YOU WILL BE REGULAR

INDIAN RESTAURANT

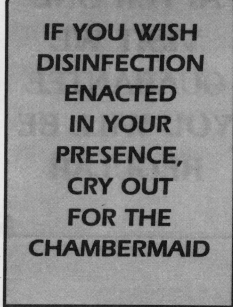

IF YOU WISH
DISINFECTION
ENACTED
IN YOUR
PRESENCE,
CRY OUT
FOR THE
CHAMBERMAID

MADRID HOTEL

**STOP:
DRIVE
SIDEWAYS**

DETOUR SIGN IN JAPAN

HAIRCUTS HALF PRICE TODAY. ONLY ONE PER CUSTOMER

HAIRDRESSER

IF THIS IS YOUR FIRST VISIT TO THE U.S.S.R. YOU ARE WELCOME TO IT

MOSCOW HOTEL

IT IS FORBIDDEN TO ENTER A WOMAN EVEN A FOREIGNER IF DRESSED AS A MAN

PLEASE DO NOT
TURN ON TV
EXCEPT IN USE

BOARDING-HOUSE

WE TAKE YOUR BAGS AND SEND THEM IN ALL DIRECTIONS

COPENHAGEN AIRLINE TICKET OFFICE

**LADIES
GET FRESH
IN HERE**

BAKERY

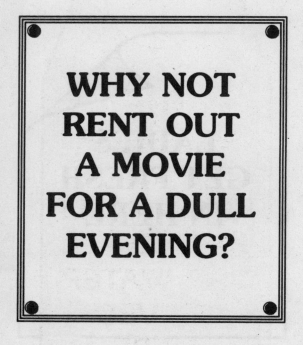

WHY NOT RENT OUT A MOVIE FOR A DULL EVENING?

VIDEO SHOP

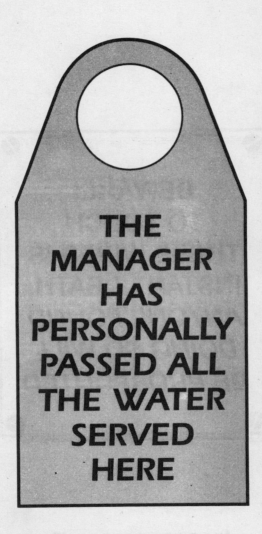

THE
MANAGER
HAS
PERSONALLY
PASSED ALL
THE WATER
SERVED
HERE

Acupulco hotel

**BEWARE!
TO TOUCH
THESE WIRES IS
INSTANT DEATH.
*ANYONE FOUND
DOING SO WILL
BE PROSECUTED***

AT A RAILROAD STATION, USA

DECORATOR
SPECIALISES IN
INFERIOR WORK.
ESTIMATES FREE

ADVERT IN NEWSAGENT'S WINDOW

SPEND YOUR
HONEYMOON
WITH US AND WE
WILL GUARANTEE
IT IS THE BEST
YOU EVER HAD

CARIBBEAN HOTEL

PLEASE
LEAVE
YOUR
VALUES
AT THE
FRONT
DESK

PARIS HOTEL

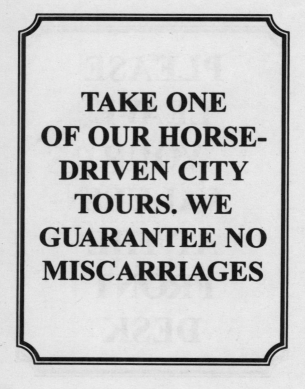

**TAKE ONE
OF OUR HORSE-
DRIVEN CITY
TOURS. WE
GUARANTEE NO
MISCARRIAGES**

CZECH TOURIST AGENCY

MEMBERS AND NON-MEMBERS ONLY

SIGN OUTSIDE MEXICAN DISCO

PLEASE
DO NOT FEED
THE ANIMALS.
If you have any suitable food, give it to the guard on duty

BUDAPEST ZOO

SCHOOL CHAPEL.
NOT TO BE TAKEN AWAY

ALL FIRE EXTINGUISHERS MUST BE EXAMINED AT LEAST TEN DAYS BEFORE ANY FIRE

HOTEL

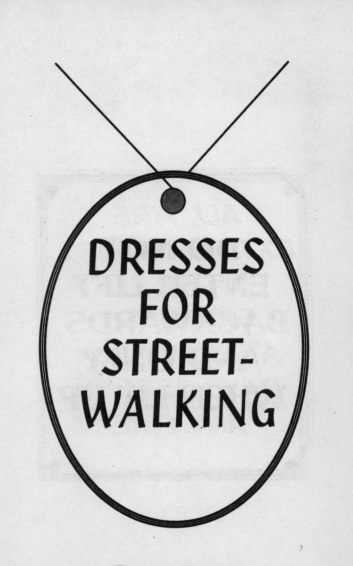

DRESSES FOR STREET-WALKING

PARIS DRESS SHOP

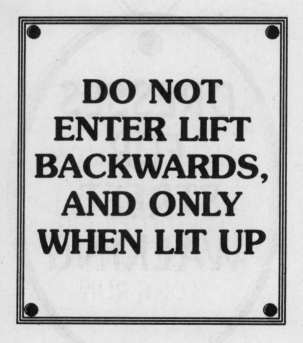

DO NOT ENTER LIFT BACKWARDS, AND ONLY WHEN LIT UP

GERMAN HOTEL

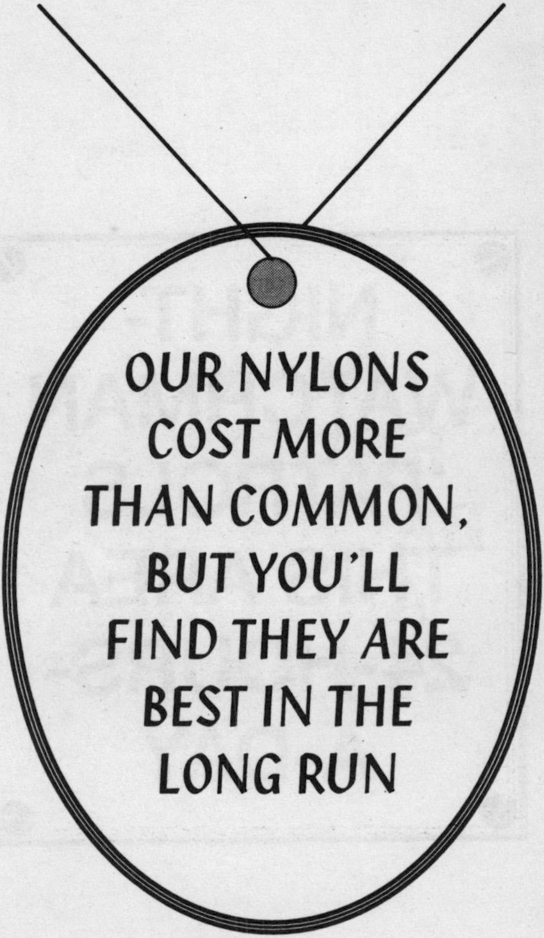

OUR NYLONS
COST MORE
THAN COMMON,
BUT YOU'LL
FIND THEY ARE
BEST IN THE
LONG RUN

SPANISH SHOP

NIGHT-WATCHMAN PATROLS THIS AREA 24-HOURS-A-DAY

BUILDING SITE

WE HIGHLY RECOMMEND THE HOTEL TART

TORREMOLINOS HOTEL

REPLACING BATTERY:
REPLACE THE OLD BATTERY WITH A NEW ONE

DIRECTIONS FOR MOSQUITO REPELLENT

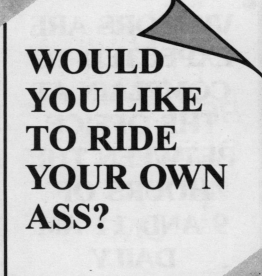

WOULD
YOU LIKE
TO RIDE
YOUR OWN
ASS?

ADVERT FOR DONKEY RIDES IN THAILAND

VISITORS ARE EXPECTED TO COMPLAIN AT THE OFFICE BETWEEN THE HOURS OF 9 AND 11 AM DAILY

ATHENS HOTEL

NO EXIT FOR BOYS EXCEPT FOR DISPOSAL OR RUBBISH

SCHOOL NOTICE

WE
DISPENSE
WITH
ACCURACY

CHEMIST

PLEASE
HANG YOUR
ORDER
BEFORE
RETIRING
ON YOUR
DOORKNOB

ANAKARA HOTEL

GENTS' TROUSERS SLASHED

DRAPERY SHOP

GUESTS ARE PROHIBITED FROM WALKING AROUND THE LOBBY IN LARGE GROUPS IN THE NUDE

HAVANAH HOTEL

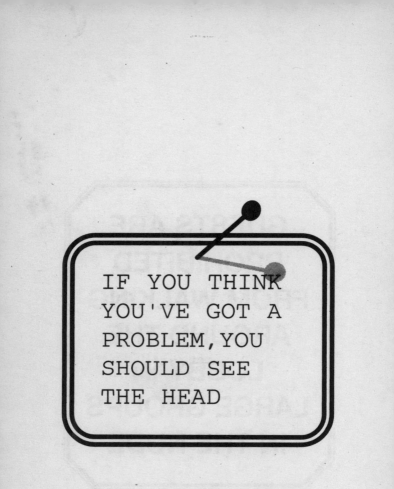

IF YOU THINK YOU'VE GOT A PROBLEM, YOU SHOULD SEE THE HEAD

STAFF ROOM NOTICE BOARD

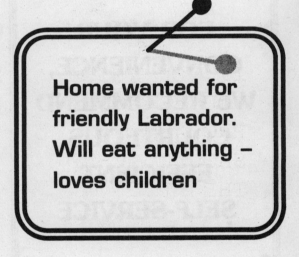

Home wanted for friendly Labrador. Will eat anything – loves children

ADVERT POSTED IN SHOP WINDOW

**FOR YOUR
CONVENIENCE,
WE RECOMMEND
COURTEOUS,
EFFICIENT
SELF-SERVICE**

HONG KONG SUPERMARKET

**OUR GIFTS
WILL NOT
LAST LONG AT
THESE PRICES**

JEWELLERY SHOP

Salad's a firm's own make;
Limpid red beet soup with
cheesy dumplings in the
form of a finger;
Roasted Duck let loose;
Beef Rashers beaten up
in the country
people's fashion

POLISH RESTAURANT

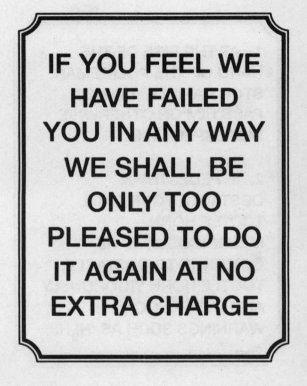

IF YOU FEEL WE
HAVE FAILED
YOU IN ANY WAY
WE SHALL BE
ONLY TOO
PLEASED TO DO
IT AGAIN AT NO
EXTRA CHARGE

DRY CLEANERS

1. AT THE RISE OF THE HAND OF THE POLICEMAN, STOP RAPIDLY. DO NOT PASS HIM OR OTHERWISE DISRESPECT HIM.

2. IF PEDESTRIAN OBSTACLE YOUR PATH, TOOTLE HORN MELODIOUSLY. IF HE CONTINUE TO OBSTACLE, TOOTLE HORN VIGOROUSLY AND UTTER VOCAL WARNINGS SUCH AS 'HI,HI'.

NOTICE OF OFFICIAL JAPANESE GUIDELINES FOR ENGLISH-SPEAKING DRIVERS

**ENGLISH WELL
TALKING HERE
SPEECHING
AMERICAN**

SIGN IN A MAJORCAN SHOP

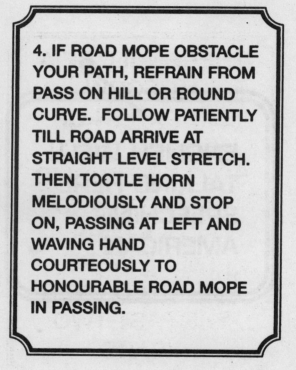

4. IF ROAD MOPE OBSTACLE YOUR PATH, REFRAIN FROM PASS ON HILL OR ROUND CURVE. FOLLOW PATIENTLY TILL ROAD ARRIVE AT STRAIGHT LEVEL STRETCH. THEN TOOTLE HORN MELODIOUSLY AND STOP ON, PASSING AT LEFT AND WAVING HAND COURTEOUSLY TO HONOURABLE ROAD MOPE IN PASSING.

AND MORE. . .

THERE WILL BE A
MOSCOW
EXHIBITION OF
ARTS BY 15,000
SOVIET REPUBLIC
PAINTERS AND
SCULPTORS.
THESE WERE
EXECUTED OVER
THE PAST TWO
YEARS

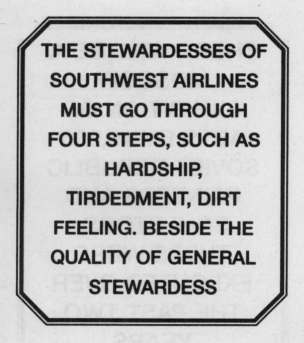

THE STEWARDESSES OF
SOUTHWEST AIRLINES
MUST GO THROUGH
FOUR STEPS, SUCH AS
HARDSHIP,
TIRDEDMENT, DIRT
FEELING. BESIDE THE
QUALITY OF GENERAL
STEWARDESS

FROM A CHINESE AIRLINE SOUTHWEST
CIVIL AVIATION'S INFLIGHT MAGAZING (SIC)

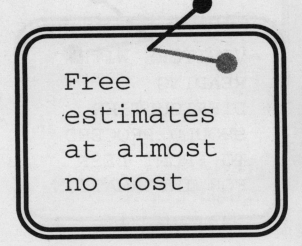

Free
estimates
at almost
no cost

GARAGE FORECOURT

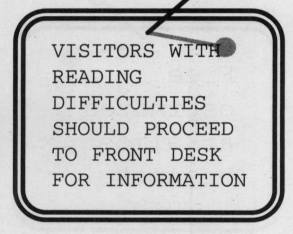

VISITORS WITH
READING
DIFFICULTIES
SHOULD PROCEED
TO FRONT DESK
FOR INFORMATION

COMMUNITY CENTRE

THE
FLATTENING OF
UNDERWEAR
WITH PLEASURE
IS THE JOB
OF THE
CHAMBERMAID

YUGOSLAVIAN HOTEL

WHEN YOU HAVE FINISHED YOUR MEAL, RETURN USED FOOD

CORRECTLY
ENGLISH
IN 100
DAYS

COUNTRY ESTATE

**CLOSED
TONIGHT
FOR
SPECIAL
OPENING**

NIGHTCLUB

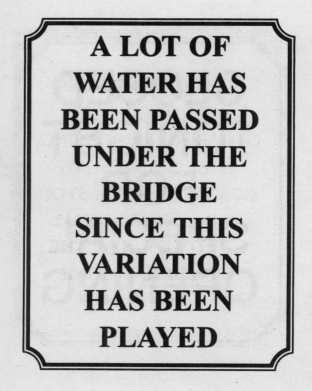

A LOT OF WATER HAS BEEN PASSED UNDER THE BRIDGE SINCE THIS VARIATION HAS BEEN PLAYED

RUSSIAN CHESS BOOK

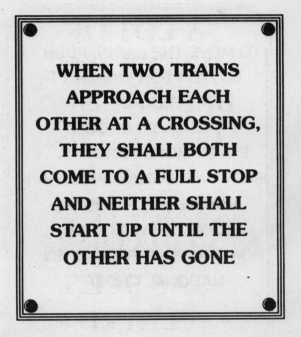

WHEN TWO TRAINS
APPROACH EACH
OTHER AT A CROSSING,
THEY SHALL BOTH
COME TO A FULL STOP
AND NEITHER SHALL
START UP UNTIL THE
OTHER HAS GONE

A LAW IN KANSAS

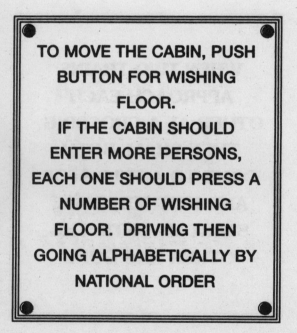

TO MOVE THE CABIN, PUSH
BUTTON FOR WISHING
FLOOR.
IF THE CABIN SHOULD
ENTER MORE PERSONS,
EACH ONE SHOULD PRESS A
NUMBER OF WISHING
FLOOR. DRIVING THEN
GOING ALPHABETICALLY BY
NATIONAL ORDER

YUGOSLAVIAN HOTEL LIFT

IT TAKES A VIRILE MAN TO MAKE A CHICKEN PREGNANT

CHICKEN ADVERT
as mistranslated abroad

Ladies may have a fit upstairs

HONG KONG TAILOR SHOP

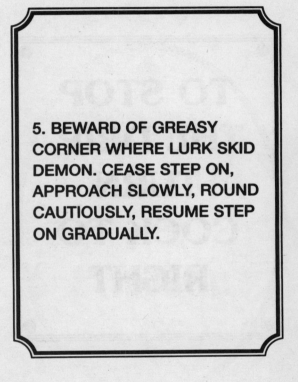

5. BEWARD OF GREASY CORNER WHERE LURK SKID DEMON. CEASE STEP ON, APPROACH SLOWLY, ROUND CAUTIOUSLY, RESUME STEP ON GRADUALLY.

AND FINALLY...

TO STOP THE DRIP, TURN COCK TO RIGHT

On faucet in a Finnish restroom

3. IF WANDERING HORSE BY ROADSIDE OBSTACLE YOUR PATH, BEWARE THAT HE DO NOT TAKE FRIGHT AS YOU PASS HIM. GO SOOTHINGLY BY, OR STOP BY ROADSIDE TILL HE PASS AWAY.

MORE FROM THE JAPANESE GUIDE FOR DRIVERS . . .

STEAK AND CHOPS ARE GRILLED BEFORE OUR CUSTOMERS

T<small>OKYO</small> <small>SHOP</small>

TO SPEAK TO A GUEST IN
ANOTHER ROOM: PLEASE
FOLLOW THESE INSTRUCTIONS:
1ST FLOOR - ADD 250 TO THE
ROOM NUMBER AND DIAL, ON
THE 2ND, 3RD AND 4TH FLOORS -
DIAL THE NUMBER REQUIRED.
5TH FLOOR - SUBTRACT 250
FROM THE ROOM NUMBER AND
DIAL, EG TO CONTACT ROOM 510
DIAL 260 EXCEPT FOR ROOM 542
WHOSE NUMBER IS 294

TELEPHONE INSTRUCTIONS POSTED
IN ZIMBABWE HOTEL

**LUNCH
SERVED FROM
12.30 TO
MID-OCTOBER**

SEAFOOD RESTAURANT

TEETH
EXTRACTED
BY THE
LATEST
METHODISTS

HONG KONG DENTIST

WEDDING GEAR FOR ALL OCCASIONS

DRESS SHOP

FUR COATS
MADE FOR
LADIES FROM
THEIR OWN
SKIN

Is forbidden to steal Hotel towels please. If you are not person to do such thing is please not to read notis

TOKYO HOTEL

LADIES ARE REQUESTED NOT TO HAVE CHILDREN AT THE BAR

NORWEGIAN COCKTAIL LOUNGE

**PLEASE
DO NOT
USE THIS
LIFT WHEN
IT IS NOT
WORKING**

HOTEL LIFT

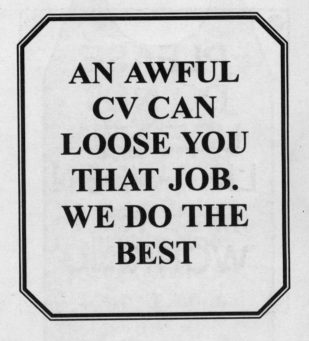

AN AWFUL
CV CAN
LOOSE YOU
THAT JOB.
WE DO THE
BEST

In order to
prevent shoes
from mislaying,
please don't
corridor them.
The management
cannot be held

HOTEL ON THE IONIAN SEA

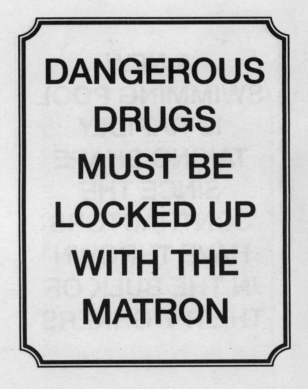

DANGEROUS DRUGS MUST BE LOCKED UP WITH THE MATRON

Hospital

A NEW
SWIMMING POOL
IS RAPIDLY
TAKING SHAPE
SINCE THE
CONTRACTORS
HAVE THROWN
IN THE BULK OF
THEIR WORKERS

EAST AFRICAN NEWSPAPER ADVERT

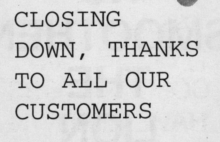

CLOSING
DOWN, THANKS
TO ALL OUR
CUSTOMERS

FACTORY

NO SMOOTHEN THE LION

A SIGN ON THE LION CAGE AT ZOO
IN CZECH REPUBLIC

PLEASE TO BATHE INSIDE THE TUB

JAPANESE HOTEL ROOM

WE HOPE YOU ENJOYED OUR NOCTURNAL EMISSIONS AND WILL BE WITH US FOR MORE TOMORROW

FRENCH RADIO STATION SIGN-OFF

AS FOR THE
TRIPE SERVED
YOU AT THE
HOTEL MONOPOL,
YOU WILL BE
SINGING ITS
PRAISES TO YOUR
GRANDCHILDREN
ON YOUR
DEATHBED

POLISH RESTAURANT

ORDER YOUR SUMMERS SUIT. Because is big rush we will execute customers in strict rotation

RHODES TAILOR SHOP

**WE NOW HAVE
SUKIYAKI
RESTAURANT WITH
LODGING FACILITIES
FOR THOSE WHO
WANT TO HAVE
EXPERIENCES ON
JAPANESE BEDDING**

JAPANESE HOTEL

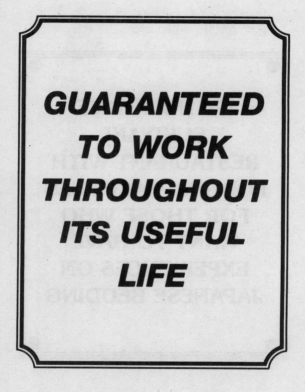

GUARANTEED TO WORK THROUGHOUT ITS USEFUL LIFE

ON BOX OF A CLOCKWORK TOY
IN HONG KONG

IN CASE OF
FIRE, DO
YOUR BEST
TO ALARM
THE HOTEL
PORTER

VIENNA HOTEL

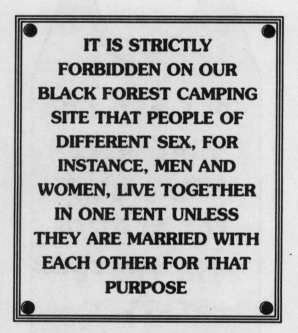

IT IS STRICTLY
FORBIDDEN ON OUR
BLACK FOREST CAMPING
SITE THAT PEOPLE OF
DIFFERENT SEX, FOR
INSTANCE, MEN AND
WOMEN, LIVE TOGETHER
IN ONE TENT UNLESS
THEY ARE MARRIED WITH
EACH OTHER FOR THAT
PURPOSE

GERMANY'S BLACK FOREST

SPECIAL
COCKTAIL FOR
THE LADIES
WITH NUTS

TOKYO BAR

SPECIALIST IN WOMEN AND OTHER DISEASES

ROME DOCTOR

COOLES AND HEATES: IF YOU WANT JUST CONDITION OF WARM IN YOUR ROOM, PLEASE CONTROL YOURSELF

JAPANESE HOTEL
(sign near air conditioner)

WE SERVE FIVE O'CLOCK TEA AT ALL HOURS

PARIS RESTAURANT

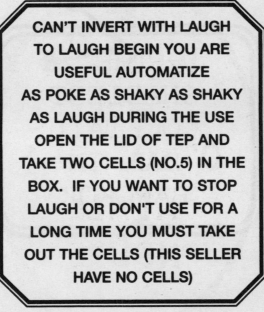

CAN'T INVERT WITH LAUGH
TO LAUGH BEGIN YOU ARE
USEFUL AUTOMATIZE
AS POKE AS SHAKY AS SHAKY
AS LAUGH DURING THE USE
OPEN THE LID OF TEP AND
TAKE TWO CELLS (NO.5) IN THE
BOX. IF YOU WANT TO STOP
LAUGH OR DON'T USE FOR A
LONG TIME YOU MUST TAKE
OUT THE CELLS (THIS SELLER
HAVE NO CELLS)

ON BOX OF A VIETNAMESE
LAUGHING TIP-TOY

THE SHADIEST COCKTAIL BAR IN BANGKOK

BANGKOK BAR

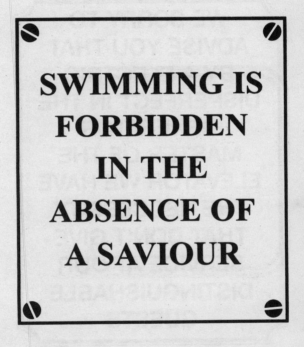

SWIMMING IS FORBIDDEN IN THE ABSENCE OF A SAVIOUR

SWIMMING POOL ON THE
FRENCH RIVIERA

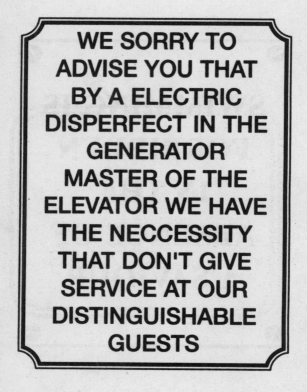

WE SORRY TO
ADVISE YOU THAT
BY A ELECTRIC
DISPERFECT IN THE
GENERATOR
MASTER OF THE
ELEVATOR WE HAVE
THE NECCESSITY
THAT DON'T GIVE
SERVICE AT OUR
DISTINGUISHABLE
GUESTS

MEXICO CITY

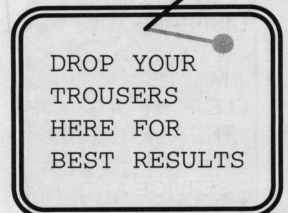

DROP YOUR
TROUSERS
HERE FOR
BEST RESULTS

BANGKOK DRY CLEANERS

TO CALL
ROOM
SERVICE,
PLEASE OPEN
THE DOOR
AND CALL
ROOM
SERVICE

ISTANBUL HOTEL

**NO SMOKING
IN THE
CORRIDORS:
THIS TRADITION
WILL COMMENCE
MONDAY**

NOTICE IN AMERICAN UNIVERSITY

LADIES, LEAVE YOU CLOTHES HERE AND SPEND THE AFTERNOON HAVING A GOOD TIME

ROME LAUNDRY

TEA IN A BAG, JUST LIKE MOTHER

PARIS HOTEL

DO NOT USE THE DIVING BOARD WHEN THE SWIMMING POOL IS EMPTY

S<small>IR</small> L<small>ANKA SWIMMING POOL</small>

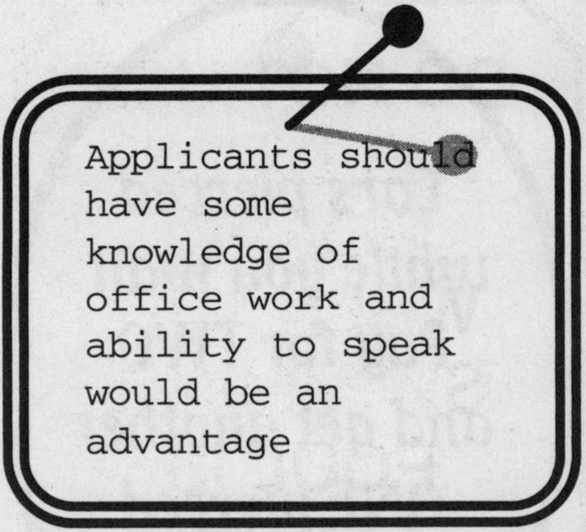

Applicants should
have some
knowledge of
office work and
ability to speak
would be an
advantage

ADVERT FOR RECEPTIONIST

Ears pierced
while you wait.
Pay for TWO
and get another
ONE pierced
FREE

BEAUTY PARLOUR

NO DANCING IN THE BATHROOMS!

GASPÉ PENINSULA

AVOID OVERSPEEDING. ALWAYS AVOID ACCIDENTS

HIGHWAY SIGN IN INDIA

BROKEN
ENGLISH
SPOKEN
PERFECTLY

MEXICAN CITY HOTEL

I
SLAUGHTER
MYSELF
DAILY

Israeli Butcher Shop

KEEP
YOUR HANDS
AWAY FROM
UNNECESSARY
BUTTONS
FOR YOU

TOKYO HOTEL

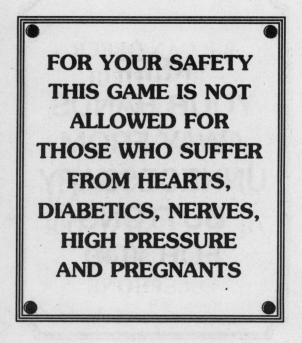

**FOR YOUR SAFETY
THIS GAME IS NOT
ALLOWED FOR
THOSE WHO SUFFER
FROM HEARTS,
DIABETICS, NERVES,
HIGH PRESSURE
AND PREGNANTS**

Amusement ride sign
in Saudi Arabia

WE CAN OFFER
A BEAUTIFUL
LUMINOUS
MATRIMONIAL
BEDROOM WITH A
CONSTANT STREAM
OF RUNNING WATER
AND USE OF
TELEPHONE

ROME HOTEL

GO
AWAY

BARCELONA TRAVEL AGENCY SIGN

A SPORTS JACKET MAY BE WORN TO DINNER, BUT NOT TROUSERS

PARIS HOTEL

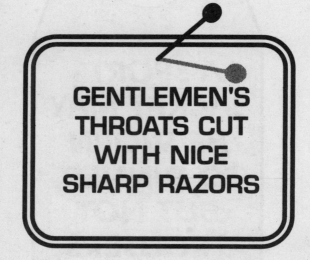

**GENTLEMEN'S
THROATS CUT
WITH NICE
SHARP RAZORS**

ZANZIBAR BARBERSHOP